CW00725750

About the au

Glen Humphries is a mult journalist. He mentions the award stop people from thinking he's jus who has no idea what he's doing. H~ ~ ~~~~ a journalist for more than two decades and has been writing books – both published and not – for more than a decade, so he hopes that he's learned a thing or two in that time. As well as this book, he's also written a few about beer, a true crime book and another about Midnight Oil. Oh yeah, there was also the collection of stories on Wollongong bands called *Friday Night at the Oxford*. You should probably visit his website (www.lastdayofschool.net) and go buy some. He's around the same age as the members of Tumbleweed and is slightly envious they all have longer hair than him. He tried to learn to play guitar. Twice. There is an electric guitar in a closet at home that hasn't been played in a decade. He is here to tell you there is no money in this book-writing caper. He will confess he's only ever been to one Tumbleweed gig in his life – the reformation show in 2009. He knows that sleeping in, like most things, is a skill you lose if you don't practice regularly. He wishes he realised that before it was too late. If you've read this far send the phrase "scooter party" to him via social media. That will be like an inside joke between you and him. Oh, how the both of you will laugh. He believes buying the CDs or vinyl rather than downloading or streaming them is the right thing to do. Creativity doesn't come easy or cheap and, if you like something, you should be willing to pay the creator something for it. Otherwise, if you keep expecting people to create music for free then soon enough, people will stop creating. And then we all lose. So stop being a cheapskate and start paying for music, writing, art and whatever other creative efforts gave you some enjoyment.

Also by Glen Humphries and published by Last Day of
School (www.lastdayofschool.net)

Healer

The Rise, Fall and Return of Tumbleweed

Glen Humphries

Last Day of School

ISBN: 978-0-6480323-8-0

To Jay, Lenny, Paul, Richie and Steve. Without whom we wouldn't have the music

"From day one the band was on a really shaky roller-coaster and there was no way it was going to make it to the end. That's my analogy for Tumbleweed."
Lenny Curley, 2008

Introduction

Looking at the story of Tumbleweed, it's hard to believe no one has bothered to make a movie about the band. As stories go, this one has it all; fame, success, top 10 hits, infighting, hubris, treachery, regret, redemption and tragedy. And there would be a killer soundtrack to boot.

In Column A there are all the good things: being signed to a US label after an exec walked into a record store and heard their single playing; scoring the support slot on Nirvana's Australian tour on the back of a promise made in a pool; releasing a top 10 album; smoking joints while sitting beside Daryl Somers' pool; touring the US and UK; a surprise reunion not even the band saw coming; and having a ridiculously loyal hometown fanbase.

Then there's Column B, the bad stuff: a messy split with your manager; getting caught up in the demise of an iconic indie label; sending the band into a slow death spiral by sacking a member; following up your most successful album with your worst; a brother who played a hand in kicking two of his siblings out of the band; and dealing with the trauma of a member's death.

The way it tended to work for Tumbleweed was that they'd get something from Column A but then follow it up with something from Column B. So they would release that top 10 album *Galactaphonic*, play all the big festivals and have people keen to see them on tour. Then, just when things were going well, when they were at their peak, they sacked guitarist Paul Hausmeister and then watched as drummer Steve O'Brien left in protest. As they would find out too late, they couldn't just replace them and keep Tumbleweed rolling along.

Sometimes it was self-inflicted. Other times the cruel hand of fate chose to intervene. In 2009 the seminal line-up of Richie Lewis, Steve, Paul and brothers Jay and Lenny Curley reunited and, in 2013, would release their best album *Sounds From the Other Side*. The band had finally managed to overcome years of acrimony and were making up for all that lost time. Then, in 2014, Jay passed away – a tragedy which rocked the remaining members and put the future of the reunited band in doubt.

Another reason to tell the Tumbleweed story is that they never really got the respect they deserved. They were generally thought of as that stoner rock band, those guys with long hair who smoke joints all day. Now, while the latter may have been true (and, in the early days, the band didn't do much to make people think otherwise), the former never was. The way the music world works is you get put in a category early on and then that's where you stay.

So Tumbleweed were dismissed as stoner rock, which missed the breadth of what they were doing. Tumbleweed songs weren't slow, thick dirges. They had swing, speed, energy, they had a groove. They were pop, they were psychedelic, they were anthemic rock, they were garage, they were old-school heavy metal (the tune *Lullaby*, released on a compilation disc in late 1992, even has shades of indie darlings Slint). People thought they were all about volume, but they could turn things down to beautiful effect (go listen to *Drop in the Ocean* and try and tell me I'm wrong). Musically, there was a lot going on in their heads underneath all that hair. It was all there if people wanted to listen, but it seemed too few really thought to bother.

While the band may have meant something to people in other parts of Australia – and perhaps the world – they meant the most to people in Wollongong. With the exception of Hockey Dad, it's hard to think of another band Wollongong has embraced so openly (and I would expect that, were Hockey Dad to break up and reform a decade later, no-one would be more excited than people in Wollongong). For years after Tumbleweed's quiet end in 2001 people would bump into one of the guys and want to talk about the band. They must have been asked about getting back together by almost everyone in Wollongong. People don't do that unless you meant something to them.

Sure, part of the reason Tumbleweed was embraced by the city was because they were successful; everyone likes to back a winner. But it was more than just being able to gloat and say "Hey, that band? They come from *my* town!", it was the message they sent to people in Wollongong. Tumbleweed (and their precursors Proton Energy Pills) showed that you could come from Wollongong and be a success. That was a huge lesson for Wollongong bands, many of whom had struggled to get even the crappiest gigs in Sydney. It told them that it could happen.

It wasn't just bands they inspired; discovering Tumbleweed was from Wollongong would give local lad Jeb Taylor the courage to start his own record labels (first High Beam and later Farmer and the Owl) and the Music Farmers record store. And Taylor would go onto repay the favour by re-releasing the *Tumbleweed* debut on vinyl in 2018.

Honestly, in some ways I'm not the best person to be telling that Tumbleweed story. You see, I was never a fan of the band on their first go-round. I knew who they were. I had friends in other bands and hung around the local scene so I'd hear their songs played at parties, see them turn up at a friend's place. But not at a gig; I never saw them play and didn't own a single Tumbleweed release until some years after they split (I did have a Proton Energy Pills single though, which I bought while *they* were still together).

A short time after the break-up, I started running the entertainment section of the local paper, the *Illawarra Mercury*. In that role I ended up interviewing several ex-Tumbleweed members about their new bands and got to know them better. Also, in time Richie became not so much "the guy who used to be in Tumbleweed" but more so "the guy who works in the same office as my wife".

Ultimately I chose to write *Healer* simply because somebody had to. I'd gotten sick of waiting for someone else to write a biography of Tumbleweed so I figured I'd do it myself. And I've lived in Wollongong since the early 1990s, so it seems the best person to write about the biggest band to come from Wollongong is someone who lives here.

After writing the feature story in 2008 that was meant to be a retrospective but proved to be a catalyst for the Tumbleweed reunion, I've interviewed the band a number of times and those interviews are used in the book. Aside from that the Tumbleweed story is told via information sourced from other interviews and articles, CD liner notes, videos and concert footage as well as listening to all the albums. There were no fresh interviews carried out for *Healer* and the band didn't know about the project until it was almost finished. The book is made up of interviews various band members have done for newspapers, magazines, TV shows and online publications – both print and video. I've also called on the plethora of videos and live footage that can be found online. Obviously, the albums, singles and EPs released by Tumbleweed – and associated bands – were also part of my research. Thanks to online purchases, my collection of Tumbleweed's music is now much, much bigger than it once was.

So, you could call it an unauthorised biography, though that tends to suggest these pages are full of scandal. I'd picked up a lot of scuttlebutt about the band over the years, but I was never interested in turning *Healer* into that sort of book. I came to praise Tumbleweed, not bury them. That said, the book doesn't dodge the tough times, the mistakes and the infighting. They are part of the band's story and it would be dishonest to skip past them. It is those darker moments that lend weight to the significance of the band's reformation in 2009. You can't really understand how unlikely that reunion was without understanding the events that created a wedge between those five members in the first place.

The reason I wrote that retrospective in 2008 was because I felt the paper hadn't paid the band the respect they deserved. There's a similar motive here; from where I sit Tumbleweed simply deserve a serious look at their career.

1

"When one looks to Wollongong as a purveyor of original, contemporary music, one is immediately struck by the sterility of the South Coast.

"While the country towns of NSW's inner west can take credit for the emergence of many of this country's better bands, Wollongong has contributed little to the national rock/pop scene."

So wrote an unknown *Illawarra Mercury* journalist in 1989. While it might sound harsh, it's a pretty accurate look at the Wollongong music scene of the mid to late 1980s. In fact, that decade wasn't a good time for the city in general. In 1982 Port Kembla steelmaker BHP – who were Wollongong's single biggest employer at the time – decided to gouge thousands of jobs out of the Port Kembla steelworks. At the start of the '80s, there were around 20,000 people being paid to make steel in Port Kembla. By the end of the decade, that number had almost been halved – and the city had to deal with the obvious flow-on effects of losing around 8000 jobs.

As for the city's music scene, well, things were a bit dire there too. A look through the gig guide that ran in the *Mercury* every Friday in the mid to late 1980s shows a mix of cover bands and variety acts, with most venues booked by Sydney agents who had little interest in putting on local bands playing their own tunes.

Yet despite what that *Mercury* article implied, there were musicians in the city fighting the tide of the cover bands. That very quote on the previous page opened a story about the EP launch for "thrash jazz" act Man Bites Dog, who had been around since 1987 (they funded the six-track vinyl EP *Life* by selling a car that trombone player Steve Fitzpatrick managed to win in a competition). The Unheard, heavily influenced by the 1960s garage sound, were also out and about – and are still playing decades later.

Wollongong in the 1980s also gave birth to Sunday Painters; guitarist Peter MacKinnon said the band played originals only because they weren't good enough to learn other people's songs. Call them what you will – pop-punk, art punk, discordant pop, electronic noise merchants – the city didn't know what to make of them. It wasn't unusual for an audience to reward them with stunned silence after each song. Yet their sound – and their DIY aesthetic (they released their own albums and EPs) – has given them a cult following that lasts to this day. A following that drives up prices of the band's original releases to triple figures whenever they appear on eBay. I'm still kicking myself that I gave away an original vinyl copy of their *4th Annual Report* album in the early 1990s because I just didn't *get* them.

Then there was this band from Tarrawanna, a northern Illawarra suburb nestled in the escarpment. It featured two of the six Curley brothers – a family apparently known to everyone in the suburb (and who possibly made up a significant chunk of that suburb's population). The Proton Energy Pills started out in the middle of 1986, with singer Lenny Curley hooking up with school friend and guitarist Stewart Cunningham. Terry Callan came on board as the other guitarist and they roped in bassplayer Michael Foy and some kid named Richie Lewis, who lived over Foy's back fence, to whack the drums.

Richie and Lenny had met before; according to the liner notes from the 2010 Tumbleweed compilation (released on Aztec Records) they spied each other at an Unheard gig at Wollongong's Grand Hotel. Fifteen-year-old Richie liked Lenny's Easybeats shirt, while Lenny thought Richie's studded belt and slicked-back hair was cool.

Anyway, it wasn't long before Foy got punted from the newly-established band, ushering in another of the

Curley clan – 14-year-old Jay. That would lead to years of having to sneak the underaged bassist into venues all over the place. The first of those was Wollongong's Ironworkers Club – the site of the band's stage debut. "We played lots of Ramones and Radio Birdman covers," wrote Cunningham in the retrospective CD collection *Rocket to Tarrawanna*, "*Sonic Reducer*, *Personality Crisis* and maybe two originals. We were terrible but it was a memorable night."

In time Callan went too, with Lenny jumping over to guitar and the band would cycle through a few singers before opting to bring in yet another Curley – older brother Dave (that's three if you're keeping score) – to take charge of the microphone.

That line-up would go onto have a lasting effect on the Wollongong music scene. Other bands would be inspired by their sound, some would see them as proof that a band from Wollongong *could* play in Sydney. Even those who passed through the Proton ranks would go on to form bands of their own, including Zambian Goat Herders, Full Tab, Leadfinger, Mudlungs, Brother Brick, the Pink Fits. And a band called Tumbleweed; though we are getting slightly ahead of ourselves.

2

Before Dave Curley joined, the rest of the band weren't taking things too seriously. They were happy to play the occasional gig in Wollongong, most of which were at parties, where covers of The Ramones, Radio Birdman and The Damned would feature heavily. Those tunes might seem tame by today's standards, where seemingly every song ever written can be heard via a quick internet search but in the late 1980s, they were very much unknown to many people.

Back then the word "alternative" wasn't just another genre; it actually meant something. You had your mainstream artists who would be the ones who you could hear on your local radio station, see on *Countdown* and get their records in the shops in town.

Then there was the spectre of "alternative music". The name actually meant something back then; it was literally the alternative to the mainstream. Records by such bands would be sold only in alternative record stores – usually tiny little stores in capital cities. People in Wollongong would catch the train to Sydney to visit them because regional record stores didn't stock alternative records – or even know how to order them in. Those records would only get played on community radio stations or Triple J, which was still just a Sydney radio station in the late '80s. On a drive from Wollongong to Sydney you'd be around halfway there before the car radio could pick up Triple J.

There was this whole other world of bands that many didn't know existed. And the idea that a band could "crossover" from those charts to the mainstream ones? Well, forget about it. That was a river no band ever crossed. Most didn't want to either; citing the evils of "selling out".

When singer Dave Curley became a Proton in 1988, it allowed Lenny to focus on playing guitar. This was the seminal Proton Energy Pills line-up and the one that decided to focus their attentions on Sydney. This was a huge decision; Sydney bands were able to come down to Wollongong to play, but few local bands had thought to step up to the big smoke.

It was a move that would pay off a year later; their bratty punk version of the Celibate Rifles' sound found an audience. And Richie's visits to Sydney's Waterfront Records to put up posters (designed by Lenny) for the band's gigs caught the attention of owners Chris Dunn and Steve Stavrakis. "They were outsiders," Stavrakis said of the band, "not part of the scene but keen. They bought records from us."

Soon they'd be making records for Waterfront. After catching a gig at Max's Petersham Inn in late 1988, the label signed up the Protons. The news made the band's home-town paper the *Illawarra Mercury* soon afterwards. Young lads being what they are, the band opted to take the piss and offer up fake names. For posterity's sake, here they are: Richard Proton (Richie), Alex Asheton (Jay), Drooper Asheton (Lenny), William Wah (Stewart) and David St Hubbins (Dave).

Cunningham remembered the night they signed thusly, "[Chris Dunn] spoke to us straight after the gig. I think his exact words were 'come and see me and we'll talk about money'."

The band was going to take its time and not rush to record their first Waterfront release. "Our following is building so we won't record anything just yet," Cunningham told the paper, "but there will be a single out mid-year and, if all goes as planned, an album to follow." He listed a few songs that were potential first singles; *Bottoms* or *Sex Farm Woman*. Yes, he was taking the piss again.

That first single – *Survival* b/w *Symmetry* – would hit the shops in September 1989 sporting a Lenny-designed cover partially inspired by the art from the Celibate Rifles' *Turgid Miasma of Existence* album.

The vinyl single came with a one-page cartoon

entitled *The Proton Energy Pills meet the Fat Bald Orbs* (plot: the bald orbs try and take the Protons' "perfect minds" for research, so the band responds by popping their brains. The end).

The A-side started off with about a minute of washed-out guitars, mumbled lyrics and cymbal work before a barrage of machine-gun drumbeats ushered in the song proper. From there the effervescence of youth is in full effect as they seem to be racing each other to get to the end of the song first. It's all speed and adrenaline. Things slowed down a bit for the B-side, a dark pop song with a few early hallmarks of the Tumbleweed sound, including a raging wah-wah pedal guitar solo just over halfway through.

The band would shoot a music video of sorts for *Survival* in the Masonic Hall in Smith Street, which had been used as a rehearsal space for bands like Man Bites Dog, The Unheard and Dave Curley's earlier band Mojo Hands. Featured in local music documentary *Steel Town Sounds*, the video shows the band playing in what looks like a half-demolished room, spending most of their time hiding behind their hair, with drummer Richie hardly even sighted.

The release would make it easier for the band to get gigs in its home town (that and the fact venues, feeling the effects of the economic downturn, decided to put on local bands in the hope of tapping into a new market). In the liner notes to *Rocket to Tarrawanna*, Cunningham remembers one show at the tiny Balkan Club in Atchison Street (where Fever nightclub is now) where the band chose to be their own support act, albeit under the name The Detroit City Cement Heads.

"We donned crazy wigs and women's stockings, entered the venue from the car park in some sort of conga line yipping and yelling throughout the venue before getting onstage to play an amazing set of high-energy cover songs." Seems the Cement Heads were too good; the crowd preferred them over the Protons.

Support slots with the likes of Dinosaur Jr and Mudhoney came in 1990; the former would reap immediate benefits, while the second would lead to an iconic tour two years down the track. During the Dinosaur Jr run of shows J Mascis was tapped to produce the Protons' second single, *Less Than I Spend*. In terms of the songwriting, it was a more accomplished effort than their debut; less speed and more space. But the production with the drums overpowering the guitars left a bit to be desired. The speed returned for the B-side *Strawberry Patch*, which sounds like it may be about being kicked out of your house and looking for a new place to rent (what with the speed and the production it's hard to pick up the lyrics).

Soon after the second single hit the shops Dave would tell the *Mercury* it was all about being slow sometimes, and fast other times. "A sense of dynamics or unpredictability, both within and between songs, is important in our music. One minute, it can be crazed and wild but in the next you can step back into something nice."

Dave also said the band was looking to "consolidate" things with the next release. But as it turned out, he should have used a different word starting with C – conclude.

3

Just over a month after those words from Dave Curley in May 1990, the Proton Energy Pills would be no more – due to those cliched "artistic differences". The band went into the studio to record an EP with Kent Steedman from the Celibate Rifles, which may have been a "we're not worthy" moment for the young fans. At least for a little while; Cunningham writes in the *Rocket to Tarrawanna* liner notes there was tension between the producer-guitarist and the band, as well as friction within the band itself.

That friction seems to be between Cunningham and everybody else in the band. Because, by the end of the recording session he was out and the Protons were done and dusted. "In hindsight it was clear (to me anyway) that Lenny wanted to go in his own direction and maybe there was some brotherly tension between him and Dave and myself because of this," Cunningham wrote.

"Throw in some misunderstood words, a bit of stress, the pressure of recording and the next thing the

Proton Energy Pills were splitting up."

The result of that final recording session would be the five-track self-titled EP (which some also call *The Sun It Shines*), which got a posthumous release in October. It would sit in the record store racks with a sticker that read "Proton Energy Pills have changed their name to Tumbleweed". Which was a bit disingenuous, because it seemed very much like a break-up not a name change. Anyway, for my money, the EP contains the best song The Protons released – *The Ride*. It opens with a long period of fuzzed out heavy guitars, which seems to give a hint as to what Tumbleweed will become (though, ironically, the music was written by Cunningham, who was the only Proton never to be in Tumbleweed). The bulk of the song has The Protons' need for speed – it even seems to speed up out of time in places. Like the rest of the EP, it benefits from better production values than the singles. It doesn't sound compressed or muddy; it's clean, clear and – especially in the case of *The Ride* – worth turning up the volume.

The Proton Energy Pills would play their last gig in Wollongong at the North Gong Hotel on July 4, which was Independence Day, ironically enough. And this new band called Tumbleweed, well, rather than go straight out and play shows, they locked themselves in the practice room at the back of the Curleys'

Tarrawanna house and rehearsed for months and months. Which is a bit odd when you think about it; they'd all been in the same band for years, hadn't they already worked out how to play together?

Tumbleweed's first gigs were in December 1990, one of which was in their Wollongong home town on December 20 (at Chequers nightclub, which was on top of Piccadilly at the western edge of the Wollongong CBD). In a *Mercury* story that month Dave Curley would explain the difference between Protons and Tumbleweed (the same story would highlight that the drummer Richie Proton would now be known as Richie Tumble).

"Obviously Tumbleweed is an extension of the Proton Energy Pills, but at the same time, we've grown up. The Proton Energy Pills were five young guys in their first band playing as fast and hectic as they could.

"Now I guess what we're doing, rather than just playing loud and fast, is putting a lot more thought into the music. It's still high energy but not as fast and more melodic."

That December would be a pivotal month for Tumbleweed. Chris Dunn from Waterfront saw an early show and loved them – "even though Richie couldn't sing," he told Craig Matheson for his book *The Sell-in*, "I was blown away". So they became a Waterfront band, but there was hardly any doubt whether the label who signed the Protons was going to pick up Tumbleweed. In a conflict of interest Dunn the label man would also become Dunn the Tumbleweed manager, which would make it hard were the band's and the label's interests to clash. As it was, the pairing would ultimately contribute to the end of Waterfront.

December was also the month they found another guitarist in the form of Paul Hausmeister. He'd been doing time in The Unheard but had been tiring of that band's rigid adherence to a '60s garage sound. His latest batch of songs for the band had been influenced by what he'd been listening to on the SubPop and SST labels, but The Unheard decided those songs would remain, well, unheard.

With that playing on his mind, Hausmeister headed to Bondi Pavilion for what has gone down in history as Tumbleweed's first official show (though it probably wasn't). And was blown away.

"Tumbleweed were playing the same stuff that was floating around in my head," he told journalist Kate Hennessy. "Their commitment and power was intense. I knew The Unheard wasn't going to gravitate towards this type of music. But here were these guys taking the bull by the horns and running off into the distance."

Figuring Jay to be the easiest mark, Paul

approached him and said he wanted to be the band's second guitarist. A few minutes later, he was. Still, it was too late for Paul to appear on Tumbleweed's first release – the seven-inch single *Captain's Log* (produced by Mudhoney's Mark Arm while on an Australian tour in December). That release would feature Dave on vocals, Lenny on guitar, Jay on bass and drummer Richie – the only time the band would record as a fourpiece.

But the single, well, it really didn't sound that much like what we now know as Tumbleweed.

4

You couldn't blame Cunningham for not wanting to listen to *Captain's Log* when it hit the shops in August 1991. But if he did he might have scratched his head in confusion; "So they kick me out, break up the Proton Energy Pills, and then go and record something that sounds like The Protons. What gives?".

At just over two minutes, (though it's under two if you discount those chickens that come in at the end) *Captain's Log* still has a strong Protons' vibe – it's got pop and it's got speed. For the four band members who went their own way to make a different sound and then spent six months rehearsing, it was odd they ended up with a first single that could have easily carried the Protons name.

The B-side, *Space Friends*? Well that's a different story. With music written by Lenny and words by Dave (reportedly while in a float tank). It's slower and twice as long as the A-side and shows the very early signs of which way Tumbleweed were about to go. It also shows some heavy duty bass grooving from Jay, who was playing in a one-guitar band for the first time and apparently feeling the need to fill up some of the extra sonic space.

That single would be the only thing Dave would record with Tumbleweed. The band that would get into a habit of kicking people out started with him. Rumour has it that Dunn got in the band's collective ears and convinced them that Dave had to go. Four years later, the Wollongong street press *Independent Music Monthly* would ask him how he felt about getting his marching orders from his brothers. He remembered the early days of Tumbleweed as "a turbulent time". "Three quarters of the band were brothers and our father had just died."

"The other guys in the band saw a direction and decided I wasn't a part of that. It was hard to take at the time but after a while … I now understand and respect their decision. At the time it was really hard to take, it was really close to the bone. In the beauty of retrospect, Jay and Rich had to do that, they had to move on and that's that."

The ousting of Dave meant Richie got saddled with the job of singing, while still remaining behind the kit. The band's return to a fourpiece would be short-lived because the final piece of the puzzle that is Tumbleweed would turn up at the North Gong when the band supported You Am I. As a member of The Unheard and, before that The Stayns, Steve O'Brien had played on bills with the Proton Energy Pills. When it came to Tumbleweed he liked what he saw – except for that singing drummer.

"To be honest, he had 'frontman syndrome' even then," he told Hennessy. "I told him straight up I could do a better job drumming." For the record, Richie agreed, referring to himself as a "huge fuckin' show pony" who couldn't just sit still and play the damn drums.

After the North Gong gig, O'Brien – who is not one to shy away from pressing his point home – followed the band to a Tarrawanna house party, where he managed to convince the band to let him join.

And so the definitive Tumbleweed line-up was together. It was definitive because it was the melding of Richie, Jay and Lenny's influences on one side with the musical leanings of Paul and Steve on the other that defined the Tumbleweed sound. Without those five guys, you don't get Tumbleweed. You don't believe me, just ask Richie.

"Lenny, Jay and I came from a band that was really inspired by a lot of Australian punk rock or independent music like The Celibate Rifles and Radio Birdman and Died Pretty and things like that," he told *B-Side* magazine.

"Steve and Paul were in a band doing '60s garage called The Unheard and they were doing it very authentically. When we both joined together, at the same time Lenny, Jay and I were going through a big sort of psychedelic phase. So I think that and at the same time meeting up with Steve and Paul and bringing their garage feel [created the Tumbleweed sound]."

Also, it didn't hurt the band's image that they all had long hair.

There is footage online of an early gig featuring the seminal Tumbleweed line-up. It's from a gig some time in 1991 at the North Gong Hotel, which at the time had a long skinny band room with the stage at one end (women tended to dislike the place because their toilet was down next to the stage, which meant they had to push their way through the crowd of punters to get there).

The video shows the first two songs on that night – the instrumental *Fritz* followed by *Stoned*, both of which sound the same as the later recorded versions. Jay has already found the stance that would serve him well in Tumbleweed; to the left of O'Brien's kit as the audience sees it, his right leg is back, left leg forward, both legs bent so he can reach his low-slung bass. Throughout the video he barely changes position.

After a brief tune-up, O'Brien counts them into

Fritz, with only four band members onstage. It's an instrumental, so Richie hangs back at side stage. Paul's to the left, his face completely obscured by hair, Lenny's at stage right, partially hidden by the stage lights, which only start working as the first song finishes. Steve's up the back, having moved the lighting rig behind him out of the way of his sticks' wind-up.

After *Fritz* ends, Richie walks onstage carrying what appears to be two cans of beer. He puts one down and opens the other; as he takes a sip, Steve starts the drum intro for *Stoned*. That seems to catch Richie by surprise so he puts the can down and heads to the mic. The resulting performance is tight, confirming those months spent in the cramped rehearsal room at the back of the Curley family house.

The first recorded offering from this line-up was where what we now think of as that Tumbleweed sound showed up. That track was *Healer* – not the version that would later appear on their debut album but one recorded for the 10-inch *Fresh From the Womb* compilation that featured Tumbleweed, Crow, Nunbait and Swirl. Lenny says it was Richie's song and it helped the band find its way.

"I dug it instantly and got real excited when we started playing it," he told The Music website years and years later. "It was a revelation as to how we should approach songwriting and who we wanted to be.

"With a single song, we realised that a heavier rock and roll approach was not only more fun to play but would be harder to pinpoint where our influences came from."

There are a few differences between this version and the one that appears on the debut album – it leads off with guitars rather than Jay's bass riff, it leaves out some of the backing vocals and it has a dirty – and better – wah-wah heavy guitar solo.

Still, they're both good versions of what is a cracking song – though I do lean towards the one we hear on the album (it's a smidge slower, which shows the song's groove and swing to better effect). Steve echoes the stuttering guitar riff with his drums at the start and they lock into a funky groove as Richie comes in with the vocals. Then we move to a sort-of guitar lead, which repeats itself after each verse.

If you listen carefully you can pick out some wicked bass runs from Jay, while Steve flings out a few around-the-kit fills. And I'm not sure whether it's Paul or Lenny who reels off that guitar solo but it's great – on either version.

It's hard to believe it would take the band nearly a year to record the song for one of their own releases.

5

When you're talking about Tumbleweed, it's a subject that's got to be addressed at some stage – drugs. Specifically, marijuana. The band had always been lumped into the stoner rock category, which seemed more because of the band's recreational predilections than their music (and of course, that long hair didn't hurt either).

It's a weird thing to make a big deal of – both in terms of people writing about it and the band getting jack of answering questions about it. Really, Tumbleweed is a rock and roll band; it's pretty much part of the job description to imbibe some sort of illegal substances. Hell, it would be more of a story if *none* of them took drugs.

But still, for years Tumbleweed stories would include some reference to weed. 'It's stupid," Lenny would later protest. "I think it started because our first single was called *Stoned* – that got the ball rolling."

And he's right (though by "first" single, he means first with the new line-up). But they did smoke the stuff. And they originally wrote that single without the "why don't they all get stoned?" chorus, which was only added after the demo stage. *And* they would go onto have another hit which became known as the "Mary Jane" song.

For all their complaining about the dope-smoking references that would dog the band, Richie realised they did bring it on themselves.

"I guess we've only got ourselves to blame to some extent," he told *Juice* magazine in 1995, "what with our name and our songs and lyrics. But we don't even take that many drugs. We're just normal people. Sometimes we smoke and sometimes we don't. I don't want to talk about it too much. It's been overdone and, besides, my mum reads our interviews."

Years later Richie would give props to marijuana and its influence in the formation of Tumbleweed's sound – that and listening to Sabbath led them to look to slow things down from the speed of The Proton Energy Pills.

"When we started smoking marijuana we just slowed stuff down," he told *B-Side* magazine. "Before that we were drinking beer. We were young kids with heaps of energy and we wanted to be fast.

"When we slowed things down and got heavier and it had more of a lag and it allowed the feel just to happen."

The *Stoned* single – released in January 1992 – would mark the start of a creative 12 months for the band. They would record or release two albums' worth of material, including the three-track EP *Carousel*, the five-track EP *Weedseed* (released with a spiral-bound cover), the *Acid Rain* single and the debut self-titled album. No wonder, as we will soon see, the band felt they were scraping the bottom of the barrel when it came to finding new songs for the *Tumbleweed* longplayer. By the way, the idiosyncratically-named *Theatre of Gnomes* was also released in 1992, but as it was a combination of the *Stoned* single and *Carousel* EP, it doesn't count as new material.

The stoner rock tag was always a lazy way of pigeonholing Tumbleweed. People just picked up on the drug references, saw the long hair and heard Richie's spaced-out lyrics and the case was closed. But even in their early stuff they were borrowing influences from other places, but we all got distracted by the hair and the distorted guitars. *Carousel* is a straightforward indie pop tune, I get some Beatles vibes from that single's B-side *Millennium*; and *Healer*, well that's just got too much swing, too much groove, too much energy, dammit, to be something a simple "stoner rock" band would come up with.

In fact, years later the tag would come to annoy the band (or at least the two original members who were left) so much they would rebel against it with what was, for years, their last album.

But we're getting ahead of ourselves again.

6

Years later, after Tumbleweed broke up but before they reunited, Richie would look back on 1992 and mark it as band's golden year.

"For me the camaraderie of the earlier days was something that we never had since," he told me for what was intended to be a Tumbleweed retrospective in the *Illawarra Mercury* in 2008.

"Everything seemed to be in place and everything seemed to be almost effortless. We were enjoying creating, enjoying playing. It was on the crest, just before things really started happening. Those were the best days – the first two EPs and recording the first album."

The band were able to cram two very significant moments into that golden year of 1992. For the origins of one of them we have to go back to 1990 and The Proton Energy Pills' tour with Mudhoney. The two bands were lounging around in the pool of Melbourne's Diplomat Hotel when Mudhoney's bassplayer Matt Lukin came up with a proposal that excited the band, and probably about 600 other people in Australia.

Lukin said his flatmate back in Seattle was also in a band and was keen to come out to Australia and play. Would the Protons want the support slot? The guys said sure, and then asked who the flatmate was and the name of his band. It was Kurt Cobain and Nirvana.

Sure, today that offer seems massive, but this was back in the day when hardly anyone had heard of Nirvana. Their debut *Bleach* had just been released (through Waterfront in Australia) and they were a year away from that other album that everyone and their dog bought. But the five guys in the Protons had heard and loved *Bleach*, and they were *so* in.

A year later, in 1991 promoter Steve Pavlovic was setting up Nirvana's Australian shows. Luckily for Tumbleweed, Pav had known about the deal made in the Melbourne hotel pool and honoured it. In what turned out to be stunningly good timing for Tumbleweed and Australia (and stunningly bad timing for the US fans – and the band's record label too, no doubt) between setting up the tour and Nirvana's arrival, the *Nevermind* album went ballistic, shooting to No1 on the American charts. When they could have been capitalising on their success in the US, they were in Australia playing gigs with bands like Tumbleweed, The Meanies and the Cosmic Psychos.

Tumbleweed would play six shows on the Nirvana tour that started on January 24 and finished two weeks later on February 7. Those six shows would see Tumbleweed caught in the moment when the music industry shifted, when the barrier between mainstream music and the independent scene was obliterated. And the band members would have to answer questions about that tour in interviews for the rest of their careers.

"When they arrived, it all went through the roof," Richie told the *Sydney Morning Herald* in 1996.

"*Nevermind* had been around for about a month and the swell – you could almost see it. It was awesome."

For Lenny, Tumbleweed's career owed a lot to what Nirvana did to the music scene.

"If Nirvana hadn't existed I don't think Tumbleweed would have ever been as huge as we were," he told me in 2008.

"That whole resurgence of grunge and punk created a situation in Australia where [record label] people said 'okay, we need a band with long hair, gym boots and flannelette shirts' and we fit the bill.

"We were in the right time and the right place."

In January 1992, the right place was on the bill of a Nirvana show with a front-row seat to a slice of history. Though perhaps when you're in the moment, you don't realise its significance.

For Lenny, two years out of high school, those Nirvana shows came to mean a lot more when he got older and further away from that time, getting some perspective on the whole thing.

"Thinking back on it, it was a fantastic experience. I remember those Nirvana gigs, thinking there was something in the air. This band was one of the sloppiest I'd ever seen but they were fantastic."

As Paul noted for The Dwarf music site in 2009, there was a lot of work that went into being 'sloppy'. He said Dave Grohl and Krist Novoselic took their preparation seriously, turning up for soundchecks and making sure it was all good. Kurt, perhaps not so much. "As far as Kurt is concerned, we didn't really see him. So it's difficult to say how professional he was compared to the others. We never really saw him. He'd show up for soundcheck and then go off on his own."

That was pretty much how everyone remembered Kurt, who was suffering from a stomach problem and heroin addiction at the time. Richie remembered just one interaction before the ANU gig in Canberra, where they showed him how to bowl a cricket ball. Other than that he was whisked in and out of all of the shows.

"The other members, Dave and Krist, were really friendly," he told *HMV* magazine. "A memorable time for me was Lenny's birthday at The Palace (in

Melbourne). We had cake and Krist and Dave came across and shared it, that was really cool."

Krist also stole a roll of film from a shop at ANU, because he couldn't help himself, according to Richie.

When they did see Kurt it was onstage, and Paul said he really worked the crowd. "Kurt just had everyone in the palm of his hand. I mean, when they played *Polly*, he just had everyone in the place singing along. And obviously when things heavied up he had the masses jumping up and down. I've never seen anything like it."

For Richie, he loved standing side of the stage and watching an "awesome and spontaneous" Nirvana. "It looked like it could fall apart at any time and it was exciting for that reason."

The tour was not without its less-than-rosy moments, which included being accused by the Nirvana road crew of swiping Kurt's effects pedals. Tumbleweed were kicked out of their own band room, while the road crew went through their belongings looking for the stolen stuff.

But of course there was nothing to be found.

7

The other big deal in 1992 was signing with a US label before Tumbleweed had even recorded their first album. The circumstances surrounding the signing sounded like it came out of a movie script. In March 1992 a guy named Craig Kallman walked into the Waterfront store. He'd just sold his own label to Atlantic Records and become a vice-president of the US giant. He was sent to Australia to check out how INXS was going with the recording of their new album.

While in town he figured he'd try and get up to speed on the hip new sounds in Australia, so he asked the guys at Waterfront to play him some stuff. And they played him some Tumbleweed (the other version of the story has it that Tumbleweed was already playing as he walked into the store).

Either way, he liked what he heard and soon after that Dunn and Stavrakis from Waterfront were playing Kallman what would become the *Theatre of Gnomes* EP. Then they got on the phone to the band.

"I got a call at work on a Tuesday afternoon saying we had to get to the Hopetoun by 6pm to play a set for an Atlantic exec with the prospect of being signed," Paul told Kate Hennessy for the *Waterfront Years* compilation's liner notes.

They threw their gear in the car and raced up the F6 freeway to Sydney, where they'd been last-minute inclusions on the bill for a Dubrovniks show.

Tumbleweed played loud, Kallman liked what he heard and signed the band to the Atlantic development label Seed. The first American release would be the *Stoned* single followed by *Weedseed*. To confuse future Tumbleweed discographers, it was not the same as the Australian *Weedseed*. For the US market, Atlantic combined the local *Weedseed* and *Theatre of Gnomes* EPs and added the track *Lullaby*, which appeared on the compilation album *Crack in the Sun or Fade in the Shade*.

As you might expect, the band was fairly stoked to jump onto a US label. Paul felt it was "like all our Christmases had come at once", while Lenny was already counting his money.

"I thought I was going to be a millionaire," he said years later. "I actually believed that. At that moment I thought we were going to be right because we'd just signed to Atlantic."

Richie would tell the Wollongong street press *Independent Music Monthly* that the "guy from Atlantic" had "a great belief in us. It's a good thing."

But it would seem that good things can turn bad really quickly. Part of that was the band's fault. A five-week tour of the US and the United Kingdom was set up and Paul said the band had fun. Maybe too much fun. "We didn't play well when we toured the states," he remembered.

"It was all an experience and we overindulged. There's a level of professionalism required when you get to that level, and we didn't quite have it."

There was also the band's understandable assumption that signing with the US label meant the Americans had a financial reason to see the band become successful. This was the era of grunge, where Atlantic and others were signing up stacks of indie bands for a pittance in the hope that one of them would end up doing huge business.

"We would have been one out of 20 bands they signed with the same objective," Paul said. "And one of those 20 was a band called Stone Temple Pilots. All the label needed was one of those bands to start charting well and the others mean nothing."

Tumbleweed would soon find out they really meant to Atlantic.

8

The Wollongong music scene that they grew up in (even though they spent a lot of their time playing elsewhere) was really starting to improve in the first years of the 1990s. That was down to the actions of a few people whose efforts acted as catalysts for others to form bands – a case of "build it and they will come".

The first of those was the establishment of Redback Music sometime in the late 1980s. It was initially located in a long, skinny shoebox of a space in the mall, right next to the church (it later moved to bigger premises almost directly opposite). Owned by John Jenkins, the crucial thing about the record store was that it stocked independent releases; even local bands who managed to scrape together the cash to press their own vinyl singles and EPs would be given space in the racks at Redback.

Before this time, finding indie releases in town was nigh-on impossible. Which was why the kids from the Proton Energy Pills had to catch the red rattler to Sydney to buy their vinyl. Now teens could have their musical horizons expanded by hearing the sounds of strange new bands playing through the store's stereo, flick through the racks and see the names of groups they'd never heard of stuck on LP dividers. Some of those kids would have then looked for places where they could go and see bands like these live. Others would use it as a spark to be one of those bands.

Which brings us to the next development – the Oxford Tavern. In the very late 1980s a few Illawarra venues experimented with booking live local bands. Most notable among them was the Coniston Hotel, where The Unheard played so many times it was like they were the house band. Patchez out at the Cabbage Tree Hotel threw a few bands on and The Balkan Club and Ironworkers in the Wollongong CBD booked a band every now and then. There was also the long skinny band room at the North Gong, which mostly hosted the out-of-town touring indie acts. But there was really nowhere you would think of as THE home of the Wollongong music scene, where you could go see bands damn near any night of the week.

That all changed in about 1990 when the most unlikely music venue came to be. The Oxford Tavern at the eastern edge of the city and just two blocks from the beach, wasn't the most welcoming venue.

Well, that is unless you were looking to score drugs or get stabbed. It was that sort of pub; called the

Bloodhouse, the drugs slipped in by the ships at Port Kembla would quickly make their way to the Oxford. In 1990 musician Steve Robinson started playing there with his band A Comedy of Errors as well as booking some other local bands.

At first he had a hard time drawing a crowd; not even people he knew were game to head to *that* place. But he persisted and they eventually changed their tune. There would soon be bands on Wednesday to Saturday nights – sometimes three on a single evening. Pretty much all a band had to do to get a gig was ask; they'd get a slot early in the week and would be able to work their way up to a coveted Friday or Saturday headline slot if they were good enough. For the punters, the Oxford would become the focal point of the scene; you wouldn't just go there because a band you liked was playing. You'd go there because you knew there were bands playing, and you knew most of the other people in the local music scene would be there too. It was hard for a regular to walk into the joint and not see people they knew.

As well as giving bands a place to play and indie music fans a place to go and watch, the Oxford also allowed people to move from one group to the other. Music fans in the crowd could see the bands onstage and think, "hey, I can do that too", and soon enough they'd get their own group together and be playing on a Wednesday night. Sure, some of these bands were crap (politeness stops me from naming names), but they still helped to keep a growing scene moving forward. Around the same time, former Tumbleweed singer and youth worker Dave Curley would start up a music program at the Wollongong Youth Centre, giving bands a rehearsal space and organising all-ages shows.

A few years later, in 1993 came the street press in the form of a typed and handwritten four-page newsletter formed by folding a piece of coloured A3 paper in half. Called the *Independent Music Monthly*, it was the brainchild of Kim Waters (who would also go on to found all-ages venue Sunami in the old Ironworkers above what is now Dicey Riley's). Today, something like that would be done online in a music blog and take a whole lot less time, money and effort. But in the 1990s it was all about the hard copy; typing it out, sticking it on pages, and then hitting the photocopier and stapling machine.

By the second issue in January 1994 (with Tumbleweed on the cover) it had jumped to eight pages and was a 12-pager with a more professional layout – and no handwriting – by issue three. It would disappear two years later (having changed its name to *Zonk* for the last few issues) but the magazine gave a voice to the local scene, and showed that some people cared enough about it to put in some frigging effort to make it better.

Perhaps the most valuable part of the *IMM* was the monthly gig guide. For a long time the only gig guide for Wollongong ran in The *Mercury* on a Friday. That was handy but would include any musician who called up – which meant a lot of the time the page was cluttered with cover acts. The *IMM* kept it to original bands, and also gave listings to radio shows that supported local music as well as other artistic endeavours that might be on that month.

In just those two pages, the *IMM* would show people in the local scene just how big it was becoming.

9

After Tumbleweed got back to Wollongong from their overseas tour, they played a free outdoor gig in MacCabe Park – in the city's CBD. Organised by Dave Curley, who was working at the youth centre, Condofest was held on Saturday, November 28, 1992, which puts it just after the release of the *Acid Rain* single, but just before the debut album came out.

Also on the bill for what was a safe sex/AIDS awareness event were Steve and Paul's old band The Unheard, popular local blues act Whose Muddy Shoes and Curley's own band Zambian Goat Herders (of whom we will hear more about shortly).

In a *Mercury* interview to promote the gig Richie would say the US/UK tour was "choice" but that it was good to be home. "There is no pretention in Wollongong," he said. "No matter where we go we always say that we come from Wollongong. I love Wollongong."

A video on YouTube catches the first three songs from the Condofest show. It started with the usual opener for the period – the instrumental *Fritz* – before moving into *Healer* and then *God*. Despite the ageing quality of the recording (it was filmed on VHS) and the fact they're playing in daylight in front of a crowd prone to standing and staring, the band still sounds good.

Tumbleweed would see out 1992 with the release of their self-titled debut. Recorded in Sydney in July, it was produced by American Doug Olson – known professionally for some reason as "Mr Colson". He'd also mixed the Australian version of the *Weedseed* release.

When you put together all the band's single and EP releases, they had already put out an album's worth of material in 1992, which meant the songwriting cupboard was looking bare. Going into Festival Studios, they had a few songs that hadn't made the cut for those EPs - like *Atomic*, *God* and even *Sundial*. They were running so low, the band had to re-record *Healer* which had appeared on an earlier compilation album.

"We had to come up with some more songs," Richie said. "So there are a couple I think we rushed into, like *Starseed*."

These days albums are recorded and edited digitally, but the Tumbleweed debut was laid down on tape. That meant the editing approach was quite different. Olson would chop up various takes of each song –

saving the best chorus from this one, the first verse from that one, the guitar solo from another – and then stick each strip of tape to the wall. When it came time to create the song that would appear on the album, Colson would splice these pieces together into one whole; effectively creating a single "take" that never really existed.

In the case of *Acid Rain*, Richie remembered this caused an issue for the band. "That song in particular, we had to relearn from the pieced-together edit of the song, because it had the addition of a few bars going into a chorus and a few other things," he said.

The band was left feeling underwhelmed by the finished album. Sitting in the Atlantic offices in New York, they heard the 12 tracks for the first time. "We all wondered what to say," Richie told journalist Jeff Apter. "Should we pretend to like it?"

When the album was re-released in 2018, Richie would say the songs sounded flat when they first heard them back in 1992. "It didn't really live up to any of our expectations," he told *Beat* magazine. "We were expecting our debut album to be this big psychedelic rock and roll freakout."

He would put that down to, in part, being young and ceding too much control to Olsen. "Having had so much control over the recording of our first few EPs, we weren't used to having someone else in there.

We were young and impressionable, and we just went along with a lot of the ideas that he presented just because we'd never done an album before. We definitely gave away too much control and we wouldn't do it that way again."

There are parts of Tumbleweed that are easy to dislike. The tracks *Dandylion* Parts 1 and 2 come across as sheer album filler. Chopped out of an extended studio jam, the band was pushed by Olson to go in and add all sorts of other sounds. Lenny agrees Part 2 is far from the band's best work. "This track highlights how desperate we were to fill out the record," he told The Music website in a track-by-track look at the album.

"While it was probably fun to make, I imagine it is greeted with the fast-forward button quite a lot."

Given it's the last track on the album, the stop button is more likely.

Richie was right about the underdeveloped nature of *Starseed* and, while *Dreamchaser* had been kicking around for a while and the band liked it, it is also one of the weaker tracks on the album.

But the band seem to be their own worst critics about the album too. It might not have been a rock and roll freakout but there is a lot to like. That includes the first single, *Acid Rain*, inspired by a bass riff Jay played on an acoustic guitar after a night of tripping with Richie in the singer's backyard.

It seems telling that they chose this tune as the first single – it was as if they were trying to show people they weren't the one-trick stoner pony everyone thought they were. But was anyone really listening? Perhaps the closest the band got to a ballad, it feels like a break-up tune – and there's even some jazz flavours there. Play *Acid Rain* to someone who had never heard of Tumbleweed and they wouldn't believe you when you said they were classed as stoner rock. Because, really, they were so much more than that.

But then the band went and typecast themselves with the second single *Sundial*. Lenny would tell *Drum Media* the band wasn't too keen on the song to begin with; he had pinched the song's riff from Jimi Hendrix's *Foxy Lady*. "*Sundial* was originally scrapped," he said, "as a rock cliché, and then we needed songs, and then everyone said it should be a single, and we've played it every gig since."

It's a song everyone knows as "Mary Jane", a not-too-subtle reference to marijuana. It would climb higher on the charts than the first single – No35 compared to No88 – and become perhaps the band's most recognised song. And that's not because it sounds like Hendrix.

"It was interesting to me because anyone can play that chord progression but only Hendrix can make it sound like Hendrix," Lenny told The Music. "When we play it, it sounds like Tumbleweed."

The song also highlights how much Steve's drumming brought to the band. His drums function more like an extra lead guitar than simple rhythm-keeping. The way he plays around the kit and throws in rhythmic skips throughout is something that would be missing from the band's last two pre-break-up albums.

As it turned out, the band weren't the only ones who weren't fond of this album. Atlantic refused to release it. Instead, they chose to cut the guts out of it and turn it into the five-track EP *Sundial*, which included the title track along with *Acid Rain*, *White Skin Black Soul*, *God* and *Healer*.

Australia went for it though; *Tumbleweed* debuted nationally at No39 and would sell more than 20,000 copies.

There was another band working on a debut album in late 1992. Four school friends from the southern Wollongong suburb of Kanahooka had formed Zambian Goat Herders in 1990. After Dave Curley was punted in the early days of Tumbleweed, those guys swooped in and convinced him to join their band. It was a canny move; having a well-known face of the independent music scene (both in Wollongong and elsewhere) helped the band stand out a bit.

It may have been Curley's presence that led to the

high-energy pop band (a little like Proton Energy Pills with a slightly slower beat) becoming the first act signed to the record label started by Redback Music's John Jenkins. He saw the band at the North Gong Hotel and liked what he saw.

The band paid for the recording of the debut *Endorphin* and Jenkins forked over the cash for the artwork and pressing. "We couldn't afford to do the whole thing ourselves, it runs into thousands of dollars," Curley told Kim Waters from the *Independent Music Monthly*.

A year later, in 1994, they would follow it up with another longplayer, *Awake*, also on Redback Records (the label would also release seven other local CDs, including discs from Pounderhound and Mudlungs).

By the middle of 1994 Curley had had enough of balancing the band's gigs with his full-time job at the youth centre, so he quit. And the Curley-less Goat Herders carried on for a year before pulling up stumps.

10

The first strong sign of Tumbleweed's ability to shoot themselves in the foot showed itself on an East Coast tour in support of their debut album. In June 1992, Waterfront's Dunn had signed on as their manager. He joined the band and their girlfriends on the tour in late 1992-early 1993, which included a slot at Brisbane's Livid festival and supports with US touring act Superchunk in Sydney and Melbourne.

According to Craig Mathieson's book *The Sell-In* Dunn spent a lot of time in the Toyota HiAce arguing with Steve and Paul. "They were older and more demanding than Lewis and the Curley brothers," Mathieson wrote (it should be said Steve is no fan of the book). By the time they got to Geelong Dunn had had enough; he called the band into his motel room and resigned. "If they [presumably Paul and Steve] couldn't see what he was doing for them," Mathieson wrote, "why should he bother?"

Richie had a slightly different point of view of the Dunn dust-up. In January 1994 he told the *Independent*

Music Monthly's Ian Gostelow that the split with Dunn
– who had attended Richie's wedding – came down to
the question of just who was in charge. "Chris wanted
to take control of the band," he said, "and we said no.
He wanted every decision management-wise to come
from him."

At the time Tumbleweed were a band of two parts,
which would have created problems sooner or later.
On one side was Paul and Steve. They had jobs (they
were using their annual leave to tour), were older and
had been around the block a few times. They realised
that the best person to take care of your business is
yourself, and so they kept an eye on what was
happening.

On the other side was Lenny, Jay and Richie. Two
were brothers and Richie was as close as one. The trio
had been in the same band for six years (if you include
the Proton Energy Pills) and were seen as the focus,
both onstage and in the studio (an impression that
overlooks the considerable contributions Paul and
Steve made to the band). They were also prone to dope
smoking, which likely led to a more relaxed approach
to the business side of the band. For Richie, the
business of the music industry sucked out all the fun.
"When the money comes in," he told Mathieson,
"there are gigantic tax bills and lawsuits and people
ripping you off and it's no longer fun. That's what kills

off the initial energy, that spirit of reckless abandon and fun."

No matter who was right and who was wrong, it would need a massive effort to keep those two disparate pieces of the band together. Internal friction seemed an inevitability. As we'll see soon enough, it was an effort some didn't feel that they needed to make much longer.

On the music front, the band would release the legendary *Sundial* single (the one people think is called Mary Jane). That song had been kicking around for a while as little more than a riff and some verses before the band got around to adding that iconic chorus for the album. The single would reach No35 nationally on the mainstream charts and the band would head out to unused land at Port Kembla to film a video (today the location is off-limits to the public as it's a huge car park for the vehicles rolling off giant car carriers that stop at the port).

The B-side included three covers of US garage acts recorded by Paul on a four-track at home – The Chocolate Watchband's *Sweet Young Thing*, *Mr Pharmacist* by The Other Half and The Escapades' *Mad Mad Mad*. There was also an extra track called *48 Brain Cells* but I can find no mention of an earlier band recording that song. The fact the song is credited to "The Dandy Lion" (also the name of two somewhat trippy tunes on the debut album) leads me to conclude this might be a Tumbleweed original.

The band also pokes a bit of fun at themselves, courtesy of an old record of Paul's that features a story for kids. Snippets of dialogue from that old record thrown in between the songs on the EP show a band frustrated with not becoming famous after having played together for three weeks.

"It's like I told you, man," one says to the others, "we've got to have a gimmick like The Beatles and The Stones."

Another bandmate then hits on a winner; "say, if we all had long hair the same colour then we would have a gimmick." There might have been friction within the band but it seems the members could at least still crack a joke at their own expense.

The band had to trundle along through the rest of the year, trying to manage themselves. That wouldn't have been fun but they couldn't find anyone else to do it. Well, anyone else who wasn't dodgy. "We had a lot of crooked people coming up to us," Richie told Mathieson, adding that he knew the management change cost them a lot of momentum.

Late in 1993, the band played what was probably one of their strangest gigs; the Wollongong leg of former rugby league player Paul "Fatty" Vautin's

World's Biggest BBQ. Heavily backed by a major brewery, there were eight of the events held across NSW and the ACT on Sunday, October 10, with the view to setting the world record for the biggest barbecue. In Wollongong, the event was held at WIN Stadium — then still known as the Wollongong Showground — with a stage set up at the northern end of the football field.

The band had played at Livid in Brisbane on the Saturday and had to jet down to make the Wollongong gig the next day. Fatty didn't show up and the band was rumoured to have almost been stiffed their appearance fee. In a short segment of the show posted to YouTube, you can see a small group of teens moshing around at the front of the stage as the band runs though *God*, while behind these kids sits a whole lot of annoyed adults waiting for the much nicer bands on the bill like 1927 and Mental As Anything to take the stage.

But there would be an upside that would come late in 1994. Looking to get some new music out rather than wait for whenever they'd end up recording the second album, in December the band would release the iconic single *Daddy Long Legs*. It would become one of the band's most loved songs and end up getting their highest ever placing on Triple J's Hottest 100 list (in 1994's list it came in at No50). It also charted nationally, reaching No53.

More importantly for the band, it was a song *they* liked (so much so they would re-release it on vinyl in 2018). To them it sounded rougher around the edges, more like *them* than that debut album recorded by a US producer.

That single was produced by Paul McKercher; a producer who *got them* and who they would later call on when they needed help recording a comeback album. The three-track single was recorded on September 11, 1993 at Sydney's Studio 301 (with a pool table and pinball machine upstairs in case they got bored). While there they also laid down a few demos of songs that would end up on the next album, including *Hang Around*.

Daddy Long Legs starts out with a bit of a curveball – a deadset stoner rock-style guitar riff. But once the song kicks off it's clear they were just tricking us; this guitar-led song really swings. In fact, it's perhaps one of the best examples of how Tumbleweed songs can swing – and it ends with a little bit of a guitar freakout.

Lyrically, I think it is largely what the words suggest it's about – a spider in a web over Richie's bed. Which would make it one of the more straightforward set of lyrics from Richie. Maybe it was the marijuana or the acid or something else but a lot of his Tumbleweed lyrics seem to come from a very unusual headspace. It was something Richie may have recognised years later, when casting an eye over his early work.

"When I look back on my teenage lyrics they're pretty airy fairy," he told the *Newcastle Herald* in 2014, "and I was into a lot of esoteric 'meaning of existence' type of stuff and I was masking a lot in obscurity, trying to hide what I was going to say."

Like so many of the band's releases, *Daddy Long Legs* features cover art by Lenny – a psychedelic TV that appears to have two screens (one showing a spider and a smaller one showing the band members as five identical longhairs). As much as the music, Lenny's efforts with pen and paper helped create the Tumbleweed aesthetic with his trippy '60s style art. His love of drawing came before music; family legend has it he was drawing the symbol of his beloved Batman before he could even write his own name.

"It's something that's instinctive," is how he described his artistic bent to Dino Scatena in 2001. "It's the same as music, it's instinct. I feel like it's not something I've chosen to do, it's chosen me.

"It's something you feel you have to do. And when you don't get pen to paper or you don't write some songs or play your music for a few weeks, you get edgy and maybe even a little bit depressed."

Lenny was also likely behind the Tumbleweed fan club – known as Weedfreaks. The *Daddy Long Legs* single seems to be the first release from the band to include the fan club address (PO Box 332, Fairy Meadow, NSW, 2519). To join you had to send a $10 cheque or money order payable to "Tumbleweed". What you'd get, according an ad for the fan club, was "your very own membership card, a comic drawn by Lenny, sticker and regular updates on what's happening".

The *Daddy Long Legs* single would also end up being the last release the band put out with Waterfront. The legendary indie label – which three of the band members had been with since the Proton Energy Pills days – would turn up its toes a year later. And drama around Tumbleweed would be a part of the reason.

11

Despite any band friction, the hassle of self-management and the continuing lack of interest from their US label poking holes in their dreams of international success, Tumbleweed was still quite the drawcard on Australian stages. Especially festival stages.

In January 1994, the band joined the Big Day Out national tour, the same year the bill boasted the likes of Primus, Teenage Fanclub, The Ramones and Smashing Pumpkins. The punters liked what they saw onstage, but it was what went on backstage that had Tumbleweed excited.

"They had portable sheds out the back of the main stage and each shed was for a band," Paul told me in 2008. "They put two sheds near each other and a roof between the two so there was this common area.

"We rocked up to our shed on the first day and went inside. We were thinking 'man, can't wait to see The Ramones'. We step out of the shed an hour later and who happens to be in the shed across from us? The Ramones.

"For the entire tour we had The Ramones sharing our common area, which, for us was just out of control."

While not too many ever realised, the four faux brothers from New York were an influence on Tumbleweed. Lenny chose to play a Mosrite guitar because that was what Johnny Ramone played. He would tell *Helter Smelter* TV that The Ramones were "the band that made me believe that I could play music".

"I would have been aged between eight and 10, and there was a show called *Sounds* on a Saturday morning," he said. "I can remember vividly the first time I ever saw *Rock and Roll High School*. I remember seeing The Ramones and I remember from that moment something clicked in my brain."

Richie too would list The Ramones as a pivotal band in his musical journey. "The Ramones are the band we got started on," he told the *Independent Music Monthly* just before heading out on the Big Day Out tour. "It's the band that opened up the whole thing that there is music beyond that which gets shoved down your throat."

There was also an Australian tour as a support act for Rollins Band and their very own festival at Byron Bay called Weedstock in December – which would morph into Homebake by 1995. In between there was the infamous gig at Brisbane's Livid in October. Held under a big top, the gig went – as they say – off. Recorded for Triple J's *Live at the Wireless* (some of which appears on the 20th anniversary release of *Galactaphonic*) the sweaty crowd was hyped. Some punters were climbing the struts that held the tent up – others had managed to reach the roof of the big top to lie on the canvas and watch Tumbleweed from on high. One of those was Steve Bell, who recalled his experiences for the Double J website.

"We were lying face-down, on the top of the tent housing the main stage," Bell wrote.

"Our heads [were] poking inside the tent, where separate sections of the temporary structure aligned, the position both completely safe and pointlessly dangerous.

"We'd been watching Tumbleweed from our vantage spot in the heavens, marvelling at how from directly above you could follow the ripple in the surging crowd as the sound travelled from the front of the tent to the rear, the bodies rippling in unison like a wave pulsing through the ocean." And that was when Livid's production manager Brian 'Smash' Chladil walked onto the stage after the band had finished *Daddy Long Legs* and took the mike from Richie.

"Hello, my name's Smash," he said. "I don't want to be a fascist, but if anyone goes near the tent poles the band's going off, and there will be no more bands until everyone's down from the tent. It's not safe and there's a lot of people who could get hurt. Cool?"

A few songs later, the punters hadn't listened; some of those camped out at the top were rumoured to have taken to sliding down the outside of the tent. So after *Sundial* was done, Smash was back. "It's me again, sorry," he said in the sort of calm voice one would use when dealing with idiots whose co-operation you want. "Can you just let these guys put that pole back? Because we've got to look after the poles or we're not going to have a tent and we're not going to have a Livid and it'll be your fault we don't have a Livid, not ours. Okay?"

They must have listened this time because the show didn't stop. Richie would later tell Faster Louder it was one of the best Tumbleweed gigs, saying it was "when everything started to come together for us as a band".

"It was the first time we heard the crowd chanting 'Tumbleweed, Tumbleweed' before we came onstage and by the time we walked out the crowd was going nuts," he said. September of 1994 also saw the band head into the studio to record an album that would create an ugly situation with Waterfront Records, the indie label that had supported them as far back as when they were still Proton Energy Pills.

12

In 1982, Steve Stavrakis was working for the indie label Phantom Records. While there he'd heard an EP by JFK and the Cuban Crisis called *Careless Talk Costs Lives*. Phantom passed on the EP but Stavrakis was a fan and decided to put it out himself. And so Waterfront Records was born, with that EP hitting the shops in 1983.

From there the label signed a who's who of the independent scene – Hard-Ons, Trilobites, Happy Hate Me Nots, The Eastern Dark and a little band called Ratcat. The troubled relationship between Tumbleweed and the label started when Dunn – who had worked at Waterfront – became Tumbleweed's manager. His decision to sign the band to Atlantic before consulting with Stavrakis was the end. "Stavrakis never forgave Dunn," Mathieson wrote in *The Sell-in*, "and their work together in Waterfront effectively ended that day." Dunn tried to return to the label after the band sacked him, but Stavrakis said no.

Around this time, there were problems with

Waterfront labelmate Ratcat, which would play into Tumbleweed's own dramas. The indie threepiece had released an EP and album with Waterfront. But then bigger labels started sniffing around, trying to woo them away. And the winner would be rooArt. The loser would be Stavrakis, who took the defection quite hard.

Today, the idea of a band using an indie label as a stepping stone to the majors is not at all surprising. Back in the day it was a very different story; the "us and them" conflict between independents and majors meant the idea of crossing over wasn't seriously contemplated by anyone. But Nirvana's success sent labels looking for indie talent, like Ratcat. When that trio jumped ship, Stavrakis felt like he'd lost a member of the Waterfront family.

That would have ramifications for Tumbleweed when they asked Stavrakis to find a major label to distribute their as-yet unrecorded second album. Polydor firmed as the likely option and, according to Mathieson's *The Sell-in*, some band members started to resent the amount Stavrakis would get as part of the deal. So the band changed their tune and looked to sign to Polydor direct, which would cut out Stavrakis altogether.

The Waterfront boss was furious. "I had gone off and spent all this time working on a deal," Stavrakis told Mathieson, "and then they said 'you're not part of the deal'." Feeling like it was Ratcat all over again, he flexed his contractual muscle and refused to let the band sign to Polydor. The major ended up having to buy Tumbleweed out of the Waterfront deal.

It was all very messy, saw the end of Waterfront and cruelled Stavrakis on the music scene. "It was long and drawn-out and nasty," Richie admitted.

13

And yet, with all this drama and animosity surrounding Tumbleweed's move from Waterfront to Polydor, the band somehow managed to record one of their best albums in *Galactaphonic*. There was some pressure around Tumbleweed's sophomore release; after the surprise success of their debut everyone was sure this would be a hit. "There was an expectation that it was going to be a huge record regardless of what we did," Richie said to *100% Rock* magazine.

Even the American label got back in touch, wanting to have their say in who would record it. Their desire was basically to have as a producer anyone who'd had anything to do with a grunge album. A guy was sent over from the US to see what was happening and holed up in the infamous Pink Palace sharehouse in North Wollongong. "We would pull up milk crates and discuss ideas," Richie wrote in the liner notes for the 2015 re-release of *Galactaphonic*. "We didn't have many. We would run through pieces of songs, he would make suggestions, nothing was coming easily."

[Healer]

The American left a few weeks later and they never heard from him again. But they still didn't have any songs — "all we had was a ragtag bunch of skeleton bones of tunes held together with bits of riff," Richie said in those liner notes.

In the lead-up to recording an album the band headed into a studio to put some flesh on those skeleton bones. Taking some control seemed to get the band's creative juices flowing and songs kept coming. "Every waking hour was about the band," Richie said. "We soaked up everything around us, mixed it up in our whirlpool and channeled it into the album. The new songs were already working live and now we were ready to record this thing for real."

Some of those new songs were road-tested by the band in a series of live shows under the pseudonym of Stumblin' Jesus Mosquito. "We'd written a whole set of new songs and we needed to try them out somewhere, so rather than have people pay money to see an experimental set, we just had a different name," Lenny told the *Independent Music Monthly* just after they'd come out of the studio. "As for the name, I have no idea where it came from."

In September 1994 they ended up in Sydney's Electric Avenue recording studio. "We booked the studio time expecting to be signed to a new label by the time we went to record," Richie told Peter Holmes.

"It didn't happen in time so we thought, bugger it, we'll pay for it ourselves with some money we had in the bank." They also decided to forget about getting some fancy hotshot producer from the US, instead opting for McKercher, the man behind the *Daddy Long Legs* single.

Fourteen of the tracks recorded in the studio – usually by the band playing together, with minimal overdubs – would make the album. That included a hidden track, a cover of Pink Floyd's *Interstellar Overdrive*, which was the result of taking acid on the last day of studio time.

Once they'd signed with Polydor, the first single – *Gyroscope* – would hit the streets in December. It would reach No50 on the mainstream charts, which was a bit underwhelming for what was the first taste of a much-hyped album. The second single was April's *Hang Around*, which really deserved a higher chart position than No48 nationally. In my view it's one of the strongest tracks on the album; it's a pop song they'd taken out the back and kicked around until it was a bit rough around the edges.

The album itself came out a month later, and the result suggested Tumbleweed fans were waiting for the longplayer. The album climbed into the top 10, reaching No6. "It managed to capture this energy of the time that was really probably the peak of our career," Richie would say years later. "We were so busy and trying to find a new direction as well because we'd had a really productive first three years. That release of that difficult second album [was when] it all sort of came together for us."

Unlike the debut album, there was no filler to be found on *Galactaphonic*. As well as the excellent *Hang Around*, the banging *Nothin' to Do With the Weather*, the strutting *This'll be the End of Me* (which sounds more than a little like *Circus Sideshow*) and the blink-and-you-miss it of *Pocket Veto* (which clocks in at just over a minute) are the standouts on a rocking album. They only take the foot off the "rock-out" pedal once, with *Listless and Satisfied* – and then only for the verses. There are no slow "stoner rock" dirges here. One of the album's songs – *TV Genocide* – would even find its way to the big screen via the 1996 Australian movie *Love and Other Catastrophes*.

As for what 'Galactaphonic' means, the band included an explanation in the CD booklet and it very much bears Richie's fingerprints. "Not so long ago, in a galaxy not so far away … surrounded by space and cosmic matter, consciousness began to converge, focusing upon a point in the eye of a galactic whirlwind. Many different lifetimes and many different realities were the projectors of this consciousness, and it grew until it was drawn into the whirlwind. The chaos of the whirlwind separated the one idea into many parts of the one idea and as it was flung into space the energy transmuted into a vibration. In certain levels of density that vibration can be heard. The idea was galactic but it had now become audible. It was galactaphonic."

I have utterly no idea what that means. This sort of thing is why they called Tumbleweed "stoner rock". However, in an interview with *TV Week* to promote the album, Richie said drugs were not used in the making of *Galactaphonic*. Under the tongue-in-cheek headline of 'Tumbleweed say no to drugs', Richie claimed they were just pretending to be potheads.

"Drugs definitely didn't play any part in this record," he told journo Jeff Jenkins. "We've always had these drug connotations. But we were just trying to be funny. We thought 'wouldn't it be funny if we called this song *Stoned*?' We've copped the [drug] image ever since."

It wasn't true; Richie knew his mum read *TV Week* and he didn't want to say anything that might get him in trouble with her. Not after that time a few years earlier when she got so angry at an infamous *Rolling Stone* article riddled with drug references that she threw the issue across the room.

14

Record companies have always put forward the impression they know about music, that they know what sells. But they don't and it's been that way for decades, ever since someone at Decca Records knocked back The Beatles because "guitar groups are on the way out". Every record label ever since has signed up bands they thought were sure things, only to watch them not shift any units, while they watched bands they knocked back take off.

Hell, just look at how the labels reacted in the wake of Nirvana. They didn't understand what just happened, so they signed up damn near every indie band that looked vaguely like Nirvana in the hope one of them might strike gold. It was a scattergun approach that spoke volumes about how little the labels knew about picking a winner.

Tumbleweed's problems with Atlantic were more of the same. The band was one of a kajillion signed up as the grunge wave broke – the fact that they weren't actually grunge speaks volumes (the band reckon it was their preference for Chuck Taylors that got them over the line). The label then got their hands all over the band's debut album. The result was a too-shiny album, one with filler (some of which was created at the behest of the US producer).

After all that, Atlantic didn't like the album; instead they cut the guts out of it and released the best tunes on a six-track EP for the US market. When Atlantic heard follow-up *Galactaphonic*, they told the band to go back and record some more demos. They weren't going to release it; not as an album, an EP or anything else.

That would be the album that went top 10 in Australia, which opens with the classic *Hang Around*, which included a number of other belters, which has no filler and which was better than their debut, *that's* the one they're not interested in. Yeah, Atlantic had no idea what they were doing.

Which was likely why the band wanted to get out of the deal, which locked them into Atlantic for everywhere in the world except Australia. New manager Joe Segretto headed to New York on Polydor's dime to meet with Atlantic bosses and sort this out. But, according to Mathieson's *The Sell-In*, they dodged him and his calls for weeks. "I was humiliated in New York where I had to try and get them out of the deal," he told Mathieson, "But I succeeded." It was a record deal the band had initially thought would make them stars but it ended up doing very little for them.

But in Australia, after the release of *Galactaphonic* in mid-1995, things were going very well. They launched a national tour, taking along Spiderbait (one member of whom would later play a greater part in the Tumbleweed story) as a support. That tour was a success, with people were queuing up to get in. "This is the best tour we've ever done," Richie said to journalist Peter Holmes.

"It's good for us performance-wise when you turn up and see 1000 people waiting outside the venue, and then you walk in and see another 1000 inside the room." Though he admitted Segretto had booked them into smaller venues, which would have obviously led to those queues outside. "It was good in a way but I wish we could play to those people who'd bought the album and wanted to hear it live."

During the promo work for *Galactaphonic*, there were a few TV appearances. One was on Andrew Denton's eponymously-titled TV show *Denton*, where the host introduced them as "a band that knows how to turn its speakers all the way up to 12". The band played a live version of *Hang Around*, footage of which lives on YouTube. It doesn't sound like the best performance, but bands appearing on TV never really sound as good as they do onstage or blasting out of your stereo.

Tumbleweed would return later in the show to take part in Denton's Musical Challenge, where a band draws a song out of a barrel and then has to go away and learn it. The Wollongong band drew Cliff Richard's *Devil Woman*. The band learned the music – they did a pretty good job actually – but Richie needed the help of a lyric sheet to get through a version just shy of two minutes long.

Another TV gig – also to be found on YouTube – is the band's performance of third single *Armchair Ride* on *Hey Hey It's Saturday* ("they're big and they're with us", said host Daryl Somers in his intro). Recorded live, it's a better performance but that may have been because they were relaxed due to being a bit stoned. "Between the sound check and the performance," Richie told *Tomatrax* music magazine, "we sat around Daryl's pool.

"We smoked joints until it was our turn to be on set. They made us go to make-up. We played well, the performance was great." And there was also a rumour that Steve may have gone wee-wees in Daryl's pool.

In terms of success, 1995 was pretty good for Tumbleweed. They released a top 10 album, were playing on all the big festival stages and were even appearing on TV regularly. But it seemed to be part of the Tumbleweed DNA that, when things are going well, something happens to throw that out of kilter. At the back end of 1995, Lenny, Jay and Richie would make a decision that would send the band into a slow downward spiral.

Up until this point older members Paul and Steve had kept their day jobs because they didn't see the band as successful enough to be able to make it a full-time thing. Still, the pair would use their holidays or arrange to take leave without pay to ensure the band could go out on tour. Sometimes, that might mean playing on the weekend and having to head back to Wollongong to get ready for work on the Monday.

After the success of *Galactaphonic* the three younger members decided that, because Paul wouldn't quit his job, he had to go. So they sacked him. "I had no idea it was coming," Paul told me in 2008. "When it happened we'd just finished a tour; we'd just played Perth on a Sunday and I'd flown back for work for Monday. It was either the Monday evening or the Tuesday, I get a call from Lenny – 'dude, sorry man, you're out of the band'.

"I never had an exact reason as to why. Quite a while afterwards I heard that was it – that I wasn't quitting work."

Also in the mix was his and Steve's approach to the business side of the band. They were more likely than Jay, Richie and Lenny to quiz managers on little details and pay attention to the bottom line. "[Steve and I] were wary of the industry and probably took it a bit more seriously," Paul would tell website Smallest Room in the House in late 2009.

"We took a pretty good look at contracts and sussed a lot of stuff out. Steve would look after the budgets at the end of tours to make sure we weren't getting ripped off. The other guys kind of just rolled along."

Paul would find the sudden sacking hard to take, because he "went from playing really great gigs to not doing anything, overnight". The band's CDs all went into a box that he kicked under his bed and left there. But, as he was still living in Wollongong, the sound of Tumbleweed was something he would never be able to escape from completely.

"The only times I heard Tumbleweed was if *Daddy Long Legs* came on *Rage* or if it was playing when I dropped by someone's place," he told Smallest Room in the House. "They'd take it off really quick though because I didn't want to know about it."

Perhaps seeing the writing on the wall and realising it was now three against one, Steve quit the band too. That left Tumbleweed needing a new drummer and guitarist quickly, because they had big gigs in January 1996 – at the first Homebake festival at Byron Bay and a slot on the national Big Day Out tour. They would enlist Celibate Rifles drummer Nik Rieth and Dave Achille, a guitarist in Wollongong band Full Tab. Achille had known the band for years – he was the singer in a very early line-up of Proton Energy Pills.

The whole thing must have been a huge buzz for Achille – going from playing in front of a hundred punters at Wollongong's Oxford Hotel to the sweaty moshing hordes at the Big Day Out. There is video footage of him onstage at the Big Day Out as the band plays *Sundial* – and Achille seems to be enjoying his time in the limelight. Though he wouldn't stay there for too long.

15

In February and March 1996, the band were on the bill for Monster Magnet's Australian tour, having just recorded their new album. There would surely have been a different dynamic within the band. They'd just lost two guys who were all but foundation members of Tumbleweed and replaced them with a drummer who still kept his main gig with Celibate Rifles and an old friend who was likely a bit starstruck and unable to believe his good fortune. They were the newcomers and perhaps viewed Tumbleweed as "Lenny and Richie's band".

It would have also caused creative problems, because Paul had been one of the band's songwriters. Now, Richie and Lenny would have to shoulder more of that load, perhaps without the same level of input they were used to from a guitarist and a drummer. I can't see either Rieth or Achille feeling strong enough to stand up and tell Lenny or Richie that their songs stink.

Years later Richie would also admit the band's fame

had a negative effect on his own songwriting. "Back then we thought, 'oh such-and-such a song sold quite a few, we better try and write more songs like that'," he told the Digging a Hole website in 2010, "and what ends up happening is things become more contrived as you go on and you end up honing your art to suit what people want.

And for these reasons and others the new album *Return to Earth* would suffer.

Richie would explain the title of the third album as a reaction to where he went to while writing *Galactaphonic*. That album was "an exploration of the relationship between the mind and the universe", he told Angus Fontaine in August 1996.

"Thinking those concepts day-in, day-out takes its toll on you and before I knew it I was lost. I was way, way out there. That's when I knew I had to return to Earth and take stock of what was going on around me."

Though elsewhere in the same article, he would suggest that the songwriting was still a little 'out there'. "People will still call it 'hippy thinking' but the images used on this record have been around for thousands of years.

"Stuff like lizards and marble moons are just a

realisation that we're all part of one big organism."

Fontaine would also try and get to the bottom of Paul and Steve's absence, which had happened just six months earlier, but no one was playing that game. Lenny and Jay weren't taking calls and Richie wouldn't broach the subject. The journalist had to resort to asking new drummer Rieth what went down. "I'm not sure, man," he replied. "It's never been explained to me either."

The story also unveiled something else – a new guitarist by the name of Al Lynch. Which meant Achille had lasted barely six months. It must have been a fresh sacking because Achille is credited as playing on the *Return to Earth* album and appears in the video for the first single, *Lava Bread*.

When it comes to albums, Tumbleweed wanted to give fans value for money. They always stacked an album with tunes – three of them would have 14 tracks and the shortest would be their 12-track debut. When it came to *Return to Earth*, they went a bit too far. As well as the 14 tracks on the album, early copies came with a bonus disc of another 10 tunes. Add in the B-sides from the three singles taken from *Return to Earth*, the band had pushed out 30 tunes (though one was a cover of a Fred 'Sonic' Smith song) in what seemed a very creative spurt.

Though appearances were deceiving. *Return to Earth* would end up being the band's weakest release by a long, long way. Maybe the 30-track output was to send a message to people the band could still crank it out without Paul and Steve. Maybe it was a message the remaining members sent to themselves, to make them feel like they made the right decision in jettisoning the pair.

What they ended up with was an album that makes one wonder if the older Paul and Steve acted as a bit a brake on the creative whims of the younger Richie and Curley brothers. The 14 tracks of *Return to Earth* include an awful lot of filler; the lowest point of which is *Time Flys*. It's one minute and 58 seconds of what sounds like a ticking clock powered by dying batteries. It's hard to understand why it's even taking up album space. It's a similar story with the one-minute surf instrumental *Blessed*, which sounds like an idea that needed more work to turn it into a full song.

The bonus disc – called *Ready by Wednesday* – really missed the mark. Full of half-formed ideas, musical whims and band in-jokes, it's hard to imagine even the most dedicated of Tumbleweed fans listening to it more than once. The songwriting credits on the bonus disc suggest whose idea this was; while the tracks on the album are credited to Tumbleweed, those on the other disc go to "Leonard Curley, Jason Curley, Richard Lewis".

The album credits contain hints of a less-than-focused approach. There are two musicians credited for playing organ on different tunes, even though neither tune appears on the album (they would both turn up later as B-sides). Also, the title track doesn't even appear on the album – it's buried in the middle of the *Ready by Wednesday* bonus disc.

All this isn't to say there aren't gems here. The lead-off track and first single *Lava Bread* (which curiously is spelt as two words on the album but one on the single) is a Tumbleweed classic. "It's a song about a traditional Welsh dish made from boiled-down seaweed," he told the *Herald Sun*'s Andrew McUtchen. "It becomes this black goo which is scooped out of a pot onto toast and then eaten for breakfast." He's telling the truth, though the dish is spelt "laverbread".

Silver Lizard also had a sweet groove going, though I don't understand Richie's lyrics at all. "See like a centipede"? They're renowned for their feet, not their eyesight. *Telepathic Cat* is just a straight-out good pop song – though who knows if it's actually about having a feline read your mind – while *Meanwhile* explores '60s psychedelia. And *Niteside* gets a mention for the incredibly loud and thick guitar riff that opens the song. It sounds bigger than anything the band had recorded before; it's like Lenny ran through the riff a half-dozen times and layered each one on top of the other for the recording.

The public response for *Return to Earth* would be a step or two down from *Galactaphonic*. It debuted nationally at No11 when it was released at the end of August but fell out of the charts a week or two later. Sales dropped to around 25,000 and suggested they weren't going to capitalise on the momentum and increased profile *Galactaphonic* gave them.

It wouldn't have helped matters that they waited until late October to tour on the back of *Return to Earth*. Presumably having to get new guitarist Lynch up to speed would have delayed any live tour, though Lenny would tell an Adelaide journo the two-month gap between album release and tour was because the Australian punter was spoilt for choice.

"There were too many international acts that came through. Australian bands always have to bargain for the entertainment dollar. The opinion is 'oh, it's Powderfinger', 'oh, it's Tumbleweed', 'oh, it's Spiderbait' we can see them any time – but we can't see these internationals at all.

"There should be some sort of quota put forward about how many can be allowed into this country."

16

Lenny would come to realise much of the criticism about *Return to Earth*, while it hurt, was accurate. "The hardest thing about it was that it's a bit true," he said later. "The record was done a bit rough and hurried. When we were younger we hit it big quickly and became naïve and just slapped together records."

As you'd expect they were keen to fix things, keen to get a new album out that was better than *Return to Earth*. One that would perhaps make people forget about it. But, in another bad turn of fate, the band would spend almost half of their career waiting for people to hear this next album.

Part of the problem was band-related; they'd picked up a new drummer in Simon Cox (ex Died Pretty) and time was spent getting him up to speed. In May 1997, Jay told the *Sunday Mail* they were about to head into the studio to record the fifth album. "We've got heaps of ideas and songs but we're just now turning them into proper songs," Jay said. "The way the songs are going so far I think the album will be more raw, not as slick as the last two records."

Jay would take part in those recording sessions (which happened in early 1998) but, by the time the album came out, he would no longer be in the band. He would become the second Curley brother to be kicked out. In a sign of just how delayed the album release was, the band would go through three bassplayers – Alex Compton, Matt Houston and Phil Lally (Houston would return for what was the band's last days) – between the recording and release.

Before the band realised how long they'd have to wait for the fourth album's release, in April 1998, they released the teaser single *Fang It*. It had been recorded almost a year earlier and would not end up on the new album. The cover featured a young Lenny and Jay leaning up against a Mini; the former looking quite proud of his snazzy brown checked pants.

"I wrote the music and Richie wrote the lyrics to *Fang It* and the B-sides," Lenny said. "We wanted a couple of quality tracks on the B-sides because the album is a little way off yet."

It was more than little way off; it would be almost another two years before anyone would hear it. The other problem leading to the interminable delays was record company shenanigans. The album was recorded and ready to go by the end of 1998 but Polydor got bought out by Universal and that threw a spanner in the release schedule.

"We spent a lot of time on it and we're happy with it," Lenny would tell the *Mercury* in February 1999. "We're now waiting for the new office to get set and we'll take it from there."

The 'new office' would push them to the back of the queue where the new album wouldn't see the light of day until 2000 – two years after they recorded it. At one stage, it looked likely the album would be a posthumous release; from 1998 the band took a break. Which apparently came close to a break-up.

"We all had, like, miniature psychoses and kind of split," Lenny told *Drum Media* in late 1999. "I'm unsure about what really happened. I think that whatever happened is just so traumatic that it's just taken away from my brain and memory forever."

Richie agreed with this, telling the same newspaper six months later that "we talked about breaking up 'cause it [the wait to release the album] got so frustrating".

To try and keep himself busy, in 1998 Richie would team up with Kram from Spiderbait – a band that once supported Tumbleweed but, like a number of others, had since moved past them on the rock and roll ladder – and form Hot Rollers. The pair would release the pop single *Wickerman's Shoes* (which featured Richie's mum and grandmother on the cover) and a full-length album. They would manage to do what Tumbleweed hadn't up to that point and get an ARIA nomination (for Breakthrough Artist – Single).

Hot Rollers certainly didn't sound anything like Tumbleweed, in fact they sounded a whole lot like Spiderbait. But the side project was a clear indication of how much Richie – and Lenny too – were getting frustrated with the stoner rock straitjacket they had been forced to wear for so long.

For all its flaws *Return to Earth* had the sound of a band trying to find a new musical direction. They didn't want to totally give up the fuzzed-out, sped-up, swinging rock (the one people always mistook for stoner) but they didn't want to *only* play that. "I think for a long time," Richie told *Drum Media*, "I felt like I was pretty constricted – and I'm sure Lenny did as well – just in trying to write for a particular style and having this thing over our head that we are Tumbleweed, that we are a stoner rock band and we have these fans, they like stoner rock and we have to stick with that."

Bands aren't really allowed to grow up and change. Their fans can, but the band has to stay the same, just in case the fans want to use them as a vehicle to revisit their own youth. While Tumbleweed was never really stoner rock, they had been tagged as "that stoner band". And now it was a tag that was really starting to chafe.

Which made the long wait for the fifth album (which was originally to be called *Supernatural* before deciding on *Mumbo Jumbo*) so torturous for the band. It was the album where they'd been brave enough to challenge that stoner rock tag, to bring in a lot of different sounds and styles. They were changing, but the delay in releasing the album delayed that change from taking hold.

The first single from the long-awaited *Mumbo Jumbo* would be released in April 2000. While the band had played it live before then, *Glow in the Dark* (written by Richie with an acoustic guitar while sitting on his back verandah) would certainly highlight a different sound for Tumbleweed. "*Glow* was done very purposely," Lenny told the *Mercury*. "It is a conscious effort to be different to what we have done in the past."

And it was; it was a single with an unmistakable country-pop feel. In another attempt to shrug off their old image the scissors came out; Richie and Lenny would get haircuts. "Chopping off the hair was a liberating thing," Richie told the *Newcastle Herald*'s Chad Watson, "because it showed that we don't need it. We're trying to exist on talents alone, without the image. It hasn't really worked yet but we feel a lot better about ourselves."

While the reviewers liked *Mumbo Jumbo* and it finally got the band their only ARIA nod (Best Adult

Alternative Album in 2000, which they lost to The Dirty Three), for many fans it is their least favourite Tumbleweed album. Which goes to show people don't like it when their band grows up.

Mumbo Jumbo is a brave album for exactly that reason; it was almost certain to alienate fans but the band did it anyway. Additionally, coming as it does just months before they implode, it's an album many forget about. Which is a shame, because it really is a good album. It does have some of those rocking tunes the punters demand, but that's not *all* it has. There's the lovely and gentle *Midnight Sunshine* with its 'Beatles circa George finding the sitar and everyone finding acid' vibe, the almost hoe-down feel of *Ghostshakers*, a love song in *I Think About You* and a country-style closer complete with harmonica in *Before the Rain Set In*.

"I had just bought a Hammond organ," Richie explained about the songwriting process for *Mumbo Jumbo*, "so I was writing a lot of stuff that was completely different to a guitar-based rock song. Also, we were in separate places, writing in our bedrooms and finishing a song and taking that finished song to practice and saying 'there's a song' as opposed to all getting in and making one up on the spot."

But the relief at having the record finally released wouldn't end up being enough to keep the band going.

The tour to promote the album saw them playing in front of much smaller crowds than they were used to.

"It became a real test of endurance towards the end," Richie told me in 2008. "The good days were the good days and you tend to remember that kind of stuff. But when you're playing The Entrance on a Tuesday night to nine people and you've got a gig the next night at Taree to 15 people. You're doing the same songs, you've got a sore throat and you don't want to do it but you have to do it anyway. That's a real drag."

But there was never an official announcement the band was breaking up, no final lap of the country to let the fans say goodbye. "We didn't say anything, we just played our last gig," Richie told me in 2019. "Attendances were dropping off, record sales were down to zip. We were at a low point in our lives; we hit a crossroads and wondered 'what the hell do we do with our lives?'."

Lenny remembered the decision being made at a Wollongong University gig some time in 2001.

"It was a great gig – the place was packed," he said in 2008.

"We looked up at the wall and the date on the poster. The date was 10 years to the day of our first ever gig. So we said, 'hey, let's just call it quits', and we did. That was it. We didn't tell anyone. I don't think we even told the other guys in the band. It was just obvious that that was what's going to happen."

With that Tumbleweed was no more. And no-one in the band seriously ever expected people would hear from the Weed ever again.

17

The members of Tumbleweed would form other bands. The first were Paul and Steve, who got together and formed a band not long after they left with a name that was a dig at Tumbleweed – Group Zero ('cause Zero is a weed killer). In 2000, along with guitarist and singer Jason Betschwar and bassist Simon Dalla Pozza, Paul and Steve would form The Monstrous Blues.

The name was derived from The Beatles' movie *Yellow Submarine*; the Monstrous Blues were the original moniker for the film's bad guys the Blue Meanies. Of all the Tumbleweed-linked offshoots, it would ironically be The Monstrous Blues that would hew most closely to that Tumbleweed sound – at least sometimes.

"We're over trying to be a certain type of music," O'Brien would tell me in 2003 for the launch of their *Colourblind* album. "Years ago I was in a '60s garage band [The Unheard]. We had to play '60s garage and nothing else. We wouldn't even go as far as the '60s psychedelic side of it."

The band would achieve some level of success; most notably being included on the soundtrack for various extreme sport DVDs (which was the big thing for independent bands in the early 2000s). They also played a live set for Triple J show *Home and Hosed*, though Paul didn't get a proper chance to hear it. "My stereo blew up about two weeks before it was on," he said. "All I had was a little trannie radio to listen to, so I didn't really get much in the way of a decent sound."

In 2009, on the back of the Tumbleweed reunion, *Colourblind* and an earlier EP *High Octane* would be re-released as the CD *A Pocket Full of Moon Rocks*. Steve and Paul would also find their way back to The Unheard

After he was asked to leave, Jay would team up with former Proton Energy Pills guitarist Stewart Cunningham in a version of his band Brother Brick. Cunningham had kept himself very busy since the Protons disbanded; his list of bands included Challenger-7, Asteroid B-612 and The Yes-Men as well as his own long-running project Leadfinger (Steve would spend time behind the drumkit in 2006).

Richie had already had a Tumbleweed side project in Hot Rollers. After the Tumbleweed break-up he would appear as a guest singer or musician on friends' albums. Eventually, he would form Richie and The Creeps, with his then-wife Sharon on bass,

Tumbleweed guitarist Al Lynch and Nate Clark (ex of local pop-punkers Fugg) on drums. An EP – *Subterranean Sounds* – would follow on Richie's own Lucky Charm label. Then a connection formed with You Am I's Russell Hopkinson during the Tumbleweed days led to a deal on his label, Reverberation.

"When I was in Tumbleweed we did heaps of shows with You Am I and became good friends with them," Richie told the *Mercury* in 2005. "You Am I gave us [The Creeps] a show in Melbourne about a year ago. We were talking about it, then [Hopkinson] said, 'When you record it, send it to me'. We have very similar musical tastes. A lot of stuff that's on that label is stuff that I like."

The sound was a continuation of sorts of the new musical direction Tumbleweed had tried to forge on *Mumbo Jumbo*. The Creeps' 11-track self-titled album contained a lot of country rock/western songs with a dash of sleazy '60s garage pop.

Perhaps the band that strayed the furthest from the Tumbleweed template was Lenny's outfit The Pink Fits. Playing an urgent, occasionally punk-tinged rock and roll, their output would include the albums *Fuzzyard Gravebox* (2006) and *De Ja Blues* (2009).

But, for the people in the crowd at these acts' Wollongong shows, the band they really wanted to see was Tumbleweed. People in the band's hometown never forgot about the band from Tarrawanna. The city's second-hand record stores were testament to that continued reverence. Back in the late 1990s and early 2000s, there were a number of those stores in Wollongong and Tumbleweed releases were almost never sighted in their racks. While people may have been short of cash and looking to offload a few CDs, they would always keep those from Tumbleweed. They were too precious to sell.

Of course, that love for Tumbleweed was a curse for the members who were all doing new things. It's the lament that always frustrates musicians – 'I like your old stuff better than your new stuff'.

"When I'm playing in my new band people will come up and want to talk to me about Tumbleweed, Lenny told me in 2008. "I'm like 'can you please just get over it? I'm over it, can you please get over it?' I feel as though I've moved on whereas a lot of people haven't. I don't want to go back and talk about it with people all the time."

Later, after the reunion, Lenny would feel he had been letting the fans down by trying to avoid the whole Tumbleweed issue. "We didn't want to live in the past and grow old being reminded of a period of three years where we had some success," he told Helen Gregory in 2011. "You got the feeling they [the fans] were disappointed in you and it was awkward."

Paul would feel a "little bit embarrassed" when people would buttonhole him and rave about Tumbleweed, while Steve still get pestered even when he left Wollongong.

"Last time I was in Melbourne," he said in 2008, "I don't know how he recognised me because I don't look like what I did 15 years ago but, pissed, two o'clock in the morning, this dude walks past me and then walks back and asks 'aren't you the drummer out of Tumbleweed?'.

"I couldn't get rid of him for the next half-hour."

While the band members were all talking to other people about Tumbleweed, they weren't talking to each other. Richie certainly remembers staying friends with Lenny, but not with Jay, Paul or Steve. Small, awkward greetings were exchanged when their bands shared the same bill, but there was no serious attempt to deal with the ongoing friction and emotions that were still there years later.

Until some journo decided to write a story about them.

18

This is where things get a bit awkward, because it's going to sound like I'm big-noting myself, but this is all true. For I was that journalist.

For a while I'd had the idea to write a "where are they now" piece about Tumbleweed – the highs, the lows, what happened, what went wrong, that sort of thing. The first time I tried I couldn't get it over the line with the boss; though it did see me buy my first Tumbleweed CD, which I happened to find at Music Farmers when it was upstairs in the mall (for the record, I bought *Galactaphonic*).

I had another go in 2008 and this time won over the boss, but then faced another dilemma; how to get all the members to agree to talk. Those I knew through friends of friends – like Steve and Richie – would be easy to approach. And then, I figured if Steve did it, then Paul would too. Having never had any dealings with Lenny or Jay, either professionally or socially, they were the ones I was worried about. There wouldn't be anyone who could really vouch for me with them.

I'd set myself a rule; if one member declined I'd still write the piece, but two could end up scuttling the story. In the end only Jay wasn't interviewed in the piece, for reasons we won't go into here.

In hindsight the fact that four of the members agreed suggested they had some hope the story could mend a few fences they hadn't been able to fix themselves. I didn't see that at the time; oh sure, I joked about how it would be cool if the story led to them getting back together, but I didn't think it was actually going to happen.

And yet it did. I think there were two reasons for that. One was that the story allowed each member to discover how the others felt about what went down. To their credit, Lenny and Richie were especially honest about admitting their mistake in sacking Paul.

Now that he was older himself, Lenny understood why Paul wanted to keep his job rather than "commit to something that was under the sway of these younger, rebellious pot-smoking unrealistic people." He also realised that, in kicking out Paul, they had sown the seeds of the band's demise.

"Certain combinations of people create better bands than others," he said at the table of his Tarrawanna home. "There's just something that happens between four or five guys and you can't just get someone else in to be that other person.

"I realised that chemistry was gone as soon as we started playing live without them. But I had to stick with whatever decision had been made. I had to try and create that chemistry again. For the rest of Tumbleweed we were trying to recreate that chemistry that we had originally."

The other reason the story ended up sparking a reunion was that I called out Richie. Of all the members he was the one who seemed least enthused by a reunion. In the interviews, Paul said he'd be up for it, as would Lenny. Steve said he was interested once, but didn't think it would happen. His reasoning was that the band almost reunited a few years earlier but one member pulled out – Richie.

When I'd asked Richie about the chances of a reunion he gently dodged the question. He was also the one member who seemed to have most successfully put the band behind him, the one who felt it was time to get on with the rest of his life. The one who figured it was time to let Tumbleweed go.

It turned out I was wrong. Years later Richie would say he came to a point where he wanted a reunion as much as the other guys, he was just afraid of saying so in case the others weren't on the same wavelength. And so the story had all the other members showing their cards on the question of a reunion, except Richie.

So it was perhaps fitting that it would be Richie who would make the first move in reuniting Tumbleweed. That would happen about a month after the story was published, when Richie had a hankering for some Vietnamese food.

19

It's not there today, just in case anyone has the bright idea to start up a Tumbleweed tour of key locations in Wollongong. But in late 2009 Vietnamese restaurant Ha Long Bay sat on the corner of Crown and Corrimal streets in Wollongong, almost directly opposite what was once the legendary Oxford Hotel.

One night, Richie and his partner would walk into Ha Long Bay looking for a table. As fate would have it, the only vacant seats were just an inch or two behind Paul, who was sitting at the next table with friends. It's telling of the members' relationships at that point that, Richie only really crossed off leaving the restaurant because he knew Paul had seen him come in.

So he walked in and sat down next to Paul, who would later say to The Dwarf website that the story I'd written for the *Mercury* made him realise "everyone had grown up over the last 13 years and things have changed" and, more importantly, that a reunion could actually be a good thing.

Also in the air was the fact former manager and

Homebake promoter Segretto had contacted the band about a possible reunion for the festival's 15th anniversary. Apparently this was a bit of a standing offer year after year, given that Homebake grew out of the Weedstock festival set up just for Tumbleweed.

As Paul admitted in an excellent Smallest Room in the House piece on the band, it was still an awkward situation in Ha Long Bay that night. "Richie walks in and sits right next to me and it was like 'Fuck! Do I talk to him or what? I don't know, fuckin' hell!' We ignored each other."

After a few wines went down a few throats, and it had done its job as a social lubricant, Richie chose to bring up the story that I'd written, which perhaps went something like this.

"You know what that idiot in the *Mercury* said about me holding out on the reunion? Well, it's not true."

To which Paul said, "Oh really? Then this is something we should talk about."

Which they did; both at dinner and over even more wine back at Paul's place. They managed to sort things out and get Steve, Jay and Lenny on board. A week later they all turned up at Lenny's house, and set up in the tiny practice space out the back. "I got there first and watched everyone show up," Richie says, "and they all seemed a little bit apprehensive.

"Nobody wanted to bring up the past and

everybody was wondering whether this practice was going to be any good."

After someone asked, "so, what do we do now?", the band decided to give one of the early tunes, *Sundial*, a crack. "It sounded great, just like the record," Richie remembered. "From that moment on there were smiles on the faces and it was really good."

It was a sign; the band would end up saying yes to the Homebake spot on December 5, which would give them plenty of time to rehearse every Sunday in that cramped band room. It was there that they discovered they all felt the same about Tumbleweed; that these five guys just *made things happen.*

Paul would tell The Dwarf the rehearsals were a reminder of how the band just clicked. "The right dynamics were all there," he said. "Particularly with myself and Lenny coming up with guitar parts."

"In every band I've been with since – and I've spoken to the others and they've said the same thing – it's always seemed like a lot more effort to get a sound that isn't as good," he told me in 2009. "When we practiced it was just so effortless; it was just there, this amazing connection.

"These five individuals who are very different from each other but, when they're in the same room making music, there's a magical quality to it and I've never experienced it since."

That magic returning would be a bit of a mixed blessing for Lenny. For years his young son had been watching his dad perform in old videos on YouTube and now he would finally get a chance to see it happen for real. That was the good thing. The downside, was the likelihood of having to play *Stoned*, which had a different vibe now that the guitarist was older. "When we were 19 and had that big single, 'why don't we all get stoned', that was hilarious," he said in 2008. "That's funny when we were 19 years old but it's not the kind of thing you want to go preaching when you're 37."

Lenny would eventually make peace with that song; as later YouTube videos would show, it would in time return to the revitalised band's setlist.

In late July 2009, the band officially announced they'd reformed and would play at Homebake later that year. "The time is right for us now," Lenny told me for a *Mercury* story. "We've dealt with all our old demons and we're all very enthusiastic about getting the band back together.

"There have been tensions there over the years for obvious reasons but I think we've finally reached a level where we're comfortable with one another and we really want to have another crack at it."

There was also a tantalising detail that had to be kept out of the story so as not to affect Homebake ticket sales. That would be the fact Homebake wouldn't be the first show the reunited band would play. That would happen just over a month earlier – in Wollongong.

That first gig would be at Waves in the northern Illawarra suburb of Towradgi. It would be on Saturday, October 31 – Halloween, an apt time for a band rising from the dead. "Waves is pretty close to being a sellout," Steve said a few days before the show, "which is quite scary for our first show back."

Richie too was a little anxious about the big gig. "I'm still a little nervous about how it's going to sound on a big stage in front of a lot of people. We haven't played in front of a lot of people for a long time, so there's a few nerves about that."

On the night, after support act Babymachine had done their thing, former Kyuss and Queens of the Stone Age bassplayer Nick Oliveri walked onstage carrying a stubbie. He stood in front of the microphone and said, "It's been a long time coming, it's been too long coming. So give it up for Tumbleweed! Tumble-WEED! Tumble-WEED! Tumble-WEED!"

The band – minus Richie – then walked onstage. History (and YouTube) will record the first song

Tumbleweed Mark II performed was the old-time gig opener, *Fritz*. There are plenty of clips from the gig on YouTube, including one shot from the front rows of the moshpit. A few seconds into *Fritz*, a punter says what everyone else at Waves was thinking, "oh, wow, man!".

As the last notes of *Fritz* rang out, Richie joined the band onstage for the full band's first live song in almost 15 years – *Atomic*. Richie would remove the "Mr Peacock" line from the song, which he had never really liked. If the band was nervous, there was no sign of it. The only visible emotion was happiness. Though at the end of the gig, Richie would realise he needed to work on his fitness if they were going to do this again.

While Richie did have the gig filmed professionally, that footage is still unseen. So the only footage is the various clips posted on YouTube. There is no one video that shows the entire gig, but a setlist of sorts can be pieced together from the range of videos posted online. As well as the two songs already mentioned, there were the no-brainers like *Sundial* and *Daddy Long Legs* (during which security had to come onstage to deal with a crowdsurfer – Waves has long had a policy of not letting the punters onstage) but they also ran through *Shakedown*, *Gyroscope*, *Listless and Satisfied*, *TV Genocide* and *God*.

If Lenny had to play the dreaded *Stoned* that night,

no-one seemed to record it for posterity. I was there and I don't remember them playing that song; but I wasn't a fan and only had the one Tumbleweed album at home – so I didn't recognise most of the songs they played.

Having scored a spot on the guest-list and a pass to the after-party, I was always going to check out a show that I had some small part in creating. I kept to the back of the room all night, wanting to leave all the spots down the front to the fans who had been waiting a decade for this night.

For the longest time fans had been asking Tumbleweed, 'when are you guys going to get back together?'. Now that they had an answer to that question, a new one rose up in its place; 'what are you guys going to do now?'

20

It was a question the band would soon come to struggle with, but for the time being it was enough for the five members to be playing together again, enjoying a second chance none of them thought they'd ever have.

The vibe was better in the band this time around; partially because Lenny, Jay and Richie were older and understood Paul and Steve's stance in the early days. Indeed, now they *all* needed to be back for work on Monday morning, which meant a lot of short two-three-day weekend tours. As well as fitting in with their jobs-and-family lifestyle, it was also the way the music world had changed too — there just weren't enough venues around to build a tour where they could play almost every night for two or three weeks.

At any rate, the band was realistic enough to know there was no point in pursuing the rock-star pipe dream. "It's not the be-all and end-all like it was back then," Steve told Wollongong's Helter Smelter TV in 2012 about the changes in the band. "It was seen as a career move back then because there were major labels involved, whereas now it more suits our lifestyle. If someone's got to work that day, then tough shit, we're not doing [that show]."

For the first 12 months of the reformation, the band played gigs where and whenever they wanted, including the Sydney and Melbourne legs of the Big Day Out just a month after their festival debut at Homebake in late 2009.

Late 2010 saw the first post-reunion release of a Tumbleweed CD. It wasn't new material; rather it was a two-CD set of all the band's Waterfront releases, from *Captain's Log* through to *Daddy Long Legs*. It was the band's idea – they put out the feelers to see if anyone was interested in releasing the stuff after being hassled by fans at the merch counter after shows.

"The majority of people turning up to the counters have been asking for records, whether we have any available, particularly the early stuff," Paul said.

"It's been difficult to get the early recordings because once they'd sold out of their initial runs, they were never re-released. Waterfront, as a label, folded, and when that happened, that was it. They didn't release anything anymore."

Richie also found it a relief that the band's old stuff was now more easily available; before the re-release via Aztec Music, second-hand record stores or eBay auctions were the only way fans could get their hands on those early Waterfront releases and the band's self-titled debut. It was also boon for the younger music fans who weren't around in the early 1990s.

"The fact that it might introduce new people to our music is wonderful, that's just icing on the cake," Richie told Kane Young from the Hobart *Mercury*. "It has been accepted very well; young people are buying it and it's a really cool thing that people are discovering us for the first time."

As re-releases go, it was impressive. Unlike some compilations, which pick the best tracks, *The Waterfront Years 1991-1993* contained everything the band had released in that period. It also highlighted just how productive the band was. There were 35 tracks across the two discs; aside from the three-track *Daddy Long Legs* single, all of those were released in 1992-93. That's three albums' worth of songs in a two-year period; a hard feat for any band, let alone one where most of the members were just out of high school.

There would surely be tracks in the set that even hardcore fans didn't have in their collections, given *The Waterfront Years* includes the early version of *Healer* and *Lullaby* which appeared on compilation albums. The set also offered a far less labour-intensive way to listen to the band's early work. Rather than having to get up and flip a vinyl single or load in yet another CD, you could just put this in the player, sit back and enjoy.

The band were certainly enjoying things and *The Waterfront Years* gave them an excuse to stroll along memory lane a little bit longer. To promote the release, the band would hit the road and included a gig in Wollongong on New Year's Eve 2010 – their first in their hometown since the reformation gig in October 2009.

"The attitude's way different to what it was," Paul told me, "Everyone's taking it a lot easier. In the jam room it's just really, really cool. Apart from the really early days I don't remember the jam room being as comfortable as it is now."

For Lenny, the big difference with the band now was it became an escape from their jobs, rather than *being* their jobs. "As opposed to the early days when Tumbleweed was our life and our reality," he told the *Examiner*'s Matt Maloney, "nowadays it is an escape from our reality and life and work commitments.

"It's our therapeutic time and we're enjoying it more now. As we're no longer making a living out of it, the passion for playing is a lot greater."

It was the same deal for Richie, as he said to Kane Young. "Whereas once it was 24/7 and it became a bit of a drag, now we actually look forward to getting together and playing shows and forgetting about real life for an hour and 15 minutes."

It was also around the time of *The Waterfront Years* release that a bit of disquiet emerged within the band. Getting back together was fun, playing the hits was fun, but were they going to be nothing more than a Tumbleweed jukebox? Were they going to put out something *new*?

The band had started working on new tunes about a year after they got back together, but there wasn't any strong idea about whether they were going to do anything with them. "We've got two that are pretty well complete," Paul told me in December 2010, "and there's probably about another seven ideas that we're working on. At the moment we're not really sure whether we'll jump in with two or three songs and record just a single to get some new stuff out there or record something more."

Five months later, they were still talking about doing something, at some point – maybe. "We're waiting until we have enough good material to make a darn good album," Paul told Kane Young in May 2011. "There's no pressure if nothing comes out, that's fine, but we're slowly working towards something and hopefully it'll be cool."

The band didn't get serious until after a corporate gig some time in late 2011. Backstage, the band had a serious talk about just what the hell they were doing. "I think that during those corporate shows we were really at a crossroad," Richie said. "We either put up or shut up. We either come up with some new stuff and start being a relevant creative unit, or we stop."

Deciding they had some "unfinished business" Tumbleweed made plans to put an album out. It was music to Paul's ears, who had been recording snatches of tunes on a cassette recorder at home.

"It's just what happens, you tend to write stuff," Paul said. "I know Lenny would be the same as well; he'd spend a lot of time in his jam room on his own and twanging away.

"I think we were all getting pretty itchy about writing stuff, it's just that we hadn't sat down together and said 'let's get serious about it and let's have a point in doing it as well'."

21

After that decision was made, the five guys headed into a Wollongong studio to record at least 20 demos. The band was so happy with the result, they went ahead and booked some studio time in Sydney in June 2012. Further recording sessions would take place over the next eight months, with favoured producer Paul McKercher at the helm. The band would eschew technology in favour of recording on two-inch tape and look to keep overdubs to a minimum.

The new album would show a different approach to songwriting. Many songs on earlier albums came out of the jam room, where the band would be several nights a week. This time around, the songwriters had had a decade to write and were bringing fully formed songs into the studio.

"There was a lot of writing we brought in," Richie remembers. "I brought in *Drop in the Ocean* and a few other tunes, like *Night Owl.* Lenny brought in his batch and Paul brought in *Mountain* and some other tunes."

While they were finishing work on the album, they

would get a reminder of how things had changed for Tumbleweed. Once upon a time, they were the youngsters on the scene, but now the fans in the front row of gigs had kids – which meant it was time for an all-ages show in Wollongong.

"Friends have been asking when are we going to do an all-ages show so they can bring their kids along," Richie told the *Mercury*. "Our fanbase has grown up."

The recording and mixing for the new album finished in early 2013 but it wouldn't see the light of day until September. It was an eagerly-awaited album, the first for the iconic Tumbleweed line-up in almost 20 years. Having to live up to that weight of expectation would have surely been a concern for the band. Would the fans expect the band to sound the same as they did back in 1996 with *Galactaphonic*? That would be an impossible task, given the remaining members' efforts to break out of the "stoner rock" stereotype late in the band's first incarnation, and the fact they had all well and truly moved on musically from where they were in the mid-1990s.

And what would happen if the band tried a repeat of the under-rated *Mumbo Jumbo* and gave the fans something different? Would they write-off the band? And, say the record actually turned out to be, well, a bit crap. What would the resulting bad reviews do to the reformed Tumbleweed? Would they go back to playing the hits? Or decide that, if the hits were all people wanted, they could stay home and listen to the records?

The public got their first taste of the new album in early August, when the band released the single *Mountain* (with a video filmed at the beautiful Cathedral Rocks in Kiama). They brought their amps along and even plugged their guitars in, even though there is obviously no power source available to make any of it work.

If this was an indication of what to expect from the soon-to-be-released album, then Tumbleweed wasn't going to have to worry about disappointing anyone. With a run-time a whisker under seven minutes, it was an unusual choice as a single. Radio doesn't play too many seven-minute songs. But then again it wasn't as if Tumbleweed was chasing massive airplay these days; they were more into having some new stuff to play.

Musically it was a clear move away from any hint of "stoner" - yeah, there's a wahwah pedal but that's as far as it went. It's not fuzzed-up on distortion like some of their earlier songs. *Mountain* was an anthemic tune; it's such a "big" song that it's easy to imagine it being blasted out of huge speakers during an arena concert. Some reviewers said the song had a bit of a Foo Fighters feel; presumably because of that arena rock vibe and not because of any suggestion it had the bland, samey "quiet verses-shouty chorus" formula that Foo Fighters are known for.

There's also a breakdown midway through the song that reminds me very much of Black Sabbath playing the *Dr Who* theme – just the rhythm, not the spacy synthesizer effect that runs over the top. Once you notice this you can't unhear it. Richie's vocal delivery stands out; it has a warmth and a tone that's not there in the band's earlier material. Maybe it's a voice he found in his years away from Tumbleweed, when he realised as frontman for Richie and the Creeps he had to sing in a different way. And I'm quite fond of the line in the song, "we will think about tomorrow, tomorrow".

The album would see the light of day on September 27. Rather than lock themselves into a record contract, the band hooked up a distribution deal with Shock for what would be called *Sounds from the Other Side*.

While the title was in keeping with the Richie-inspired style of mysticism the band was known for (though by this stage Lenny had gotten into Buddhism), it was preferable to see it as a reference to the band's break-up and reformation. They'd gone through a lot of crap and come out the other side with this batch of 13 tunes.

And what a great batch of tunes they were. For many, it would have been enough for the band to release a decent album with a few good songs. But for them to go and release the best album of their career – after all that acrimony, the break-up and the surprise reformation – was certainly unexpected. Once upon a time the top 10 album *Galactaphonic* was the band's best, but not anymore. It mighn't have charted like *Galactaphonic* (and Tumbleweed were no longer the sort of band likely to trouble the charts these days) but it was unquestionably better.

It bore some similarity to *Mumbo Jumbo*, the last album before Richie and Lenny pulled the plug on Tumbleweed Mark I. Both albums found the band trying to break away from that stoner rock straitjacket. They weren't able to achieve that with back in 2000 with *Mumbo Jumbo* due to a range of factors including record company machinations, the fans not willing to let them grow and the band simply getting jack of the whole thing.

With the passage of time, the fans getting older and the band having fun again, they nailed the move to broader musical horizons with *Sounds from the Other Side*. So it's worth having a quick look at each of the songs individually.

Mandlebrot: The album starts things off with a single drumbeat before launching into a driving guitar riff. The shortest song on the album, it's a good rocking start for those still wanting that from Tumbleweed. The backing harmonies that pop up here and there are nice and subtle and there's a killer guitar solo from Paul that sounds like he's trying to choke every note out of the thing.

By the way, I'm not sure if the song has any link to the mathematician Benoit Mandelbrot, after whom the Mandelbrot set is named. What is the Mandelbrot set? Dunno, I tried to read the Wikipedia page but it hurt my brain.

Sweet Little Runaway: They take a slight diversion with the second tune about a runaway whose absence will hardly be noted back at home. The song has a bit of a '60s sleaze rock feel, with Steve changing up the beat big time between the verses and the chorus.

Mountain: We've already been through this one a few pages earlier.

Like a Night Owl: Not all of the songs on *Sounds from the Other Side* were written after the reformation. This is one of two songs on the album that were originally Richie and the Creeps tunes. Check out YouTube for footage of that band performing this song in an acoustic set at Music Farmers' Crown Lane store. It has more of a country feel than what happened when Tumbleweed were through with it.

It was the second single from the album and feels

like a mash-up of '60s garage and '70s New York punk. There's also a wicked sense of humour here in what is a song about a couple coming down after a very big night indeed – so much so that the narrator's partner has her head out the window about to throw up.

Dirty Little Secret: It kicks off with Steve seemingly trying to hit every piece of his kit at the same time. A long time ago, Richie said he liked that Steve played around the kit – and he certainly does that as this song starts. Lyrically, the song – about heartbreak and rejection – is more direct and open than most of Richie's early stuff. "With this record I've tried to be a little bit more direct and have a clearer idea of what the song is about, what I'm trying to say, not overthink it, try to be simple," he said. So it's a pity the album doesn't come with a lyric sheet so we can get a better look at those words.

Drop in the Ocean: This is the other song that was originally performed by Richie and the Creeps at that Music Farmers gig back in 2007. It doesn't sound like anything special in that version, but Tumbleweed turn it into the best song they ever released. It's a big call, I know, but it earns that title in part because it's a real change of direction for the band and they make the transition seamlessly.

It's the centrepiece of the album and, with the band's input it becomes a song that carries with it echoes of David Bowie's *Heroes*. That FM radio didn't gobble this up when it was released is an injustice. In just under a year's time, the song would get an extra poignancy with the passing of a band member.

Wildfire: This is a song that goes all the way back to the mid-1990s. Richie told Music Feeds' Mike Hohnen that they found the tune on an old demo tape and it sounded a bit like Blue Cheer. "We forgot about it but it had this amazing riff and Lenny had a great hook on the chorus."

Most of the stuff from back in the day that was resurrected for *Sounds from the Other Side* needed some work. "They were never really finished," Richie said of all those old demo recordings, "just skeletons that needed work so they sound and feel brand-new.

Hillbilly Headbanger: It's almost two songs in one. The verses – if that's what they are – have a country strut to them. Get to the chorus and there's a bit of a punk edge that calls to mind Lenny's side project The Pink Fits. Though I'm not sure where the Hillbilly bit comes in. Or the headbanging for that matter.

Queen of Voodoo: Musically, there's good-dumb and bad-dumb. Being good-dumb takes some effort. Bad-dumb? Well, that takes no effort at all. *Queen of Voodoo* is good-dumb - it's an intentionally cheesy with a swampy garage rock vibe and chants as backing vocals. The song works even better when you listen to it via the music video made by Shannon Reid (the guy also responsible for the *Night Owl* video), using artwork by Lenny. The bit where he turns the five members of Tumbleweed into an early Disney cartoon is marvellous.

Good and Evil: Paul is partial to some Status Quo and there's a bit of that UK band here – so I wouldn't be surprised if he had a hand it this tune. It sounds like there's a Hammond organ in the mix and, while there's no-one credited with that on the album, the fact Richie used one to write some of the songs that ended up on *Mumbo Jumbo* suggests it could well be him. There's also shades of ZZ Top and a whisper of stoner rock at the end.

Down and Dirty: I hear that guitar riff and it carries the whiff of '70s exploitation films or old pornos. Which I guess is the vibe they were going for, given the title of the song. It's just a bunch of fun.

Bird of Prey: One of Tumbleweed's influences was Black Sabbath, with perhaps a dash of Deep Purple. In *Bird of Prey*, those influences really stand out. It's like they listened to a few of those albums and tried to combine those bands' sound into one song – call it Black Purple.

ESP: At 7:04 minutes, this beats *Mountain* for the title of longest song on the album by just five seconds.

[Healer]

A psychedelic surf tune, it's well placed as the album closer. It's got a long, slow fade-out so you leave the album gradually rather than all of a sudden.

For Richie, *Sounds from the Other Side* would be the album he thought would never exist. "It's a record I never thought that I would be sitting here talking about," he told the AU Review just after the album's release. "I never thought that we would ever get back together. I didn't think we'd be friends again, it wasn't a nice break-up. It was something that we carried around with us like a weight. It was a big regret in our lives, what we did and how we broke up."

Sadly he would only have just over six months to enjoy the reformed Tumbleweed line-up.

22

Through late 2013 and early 2014 the band played a series of shows to plug the new album. Then, in early August came the news that Tumbleweed would headline a street festival in the Sydney suburb of Marrickville in September, organised by Young Henrys. Called Small World, it would also feature The Delta Riggs, Bloods and The Snowdroppers.

Just two weeks after that announcement, Tumbleweed would be hit by a tragedy that would not only put their appearance at the Small World show in doubt but would cause the band to question whether they wanted to keep on playing.

On Monday, August 25, Jay's body was found in the Tarrawanna house he'd moved into just a few months earlier. While there would be the inevitable rumours of a drug overdose, the bassplayer's death was the result of a long-running battle with alcohol (his problem may have been a factor in his being asked to leave the band while it was in its last throes in the late 1990s).

A day later, the band would post a message on their Facebook page about Jay. "It is with deep sadness that we inform everyone of a great loss in the Tumbleweed family, our brother, friend and bassplayer Jay Curley passed away suddenly in his home yesterday. We are still shocked by the news of his death. We hope that people will remember him for his music, his big heart and his total dedication to rock and roll."

Paul would call him "the face of Wollongong rock'n'roll", a guy with "tattoos on the outside with a warm, loving, gentle soul on the inside."

"He has inspired countless musicians over the last 30 years and will continue [to do so] into the future. The Australian rock'n'roll community has lost a great musician and a great bloke. We have lost a great mate."

Any loss of a friend and a bandmate would be devastating, but there was an extra sting for Tumbleweed. Coming just a few years after the reformation, Jay's death would cause his bandmates to further rue the wasted years they'd spent apart, all the time they'd lost. It would lead the band through a bout of genuine soul-searching, wondering if Tumbleweed could still *be* Tumbleweed without Jay. They would play the Small World festival – and three others that had already been booked – but Lenny intimated that could be all she wrote. "In all honesty, the magic of the band was in the line-up with Jay," his brother told the *Sydney Morning Herald*'s Peter Vincent. "That might suggest these will be our last shows … it might be a good time to hang up our guitars, at least for a while."

For the Small World gig on September 20, Jay's older brother Pat – who was the first of the Curleys to learn to play – would fill in on bass. Pat had to take time out to learn the Tumbleweed songs, finding things about his little brother's technique that caught him off guard.

"To get in and figure out what the hell he was doing has been interesting," Pat said on the afternoon of the gig. "I knew he could play and I knew his asset was his groove. But it did surprise me I'd have to say, his level of sophistication in his playing.

"I'm a jazz player and I can see what Jay was doing in terms of connecting lines up together and walking things. He was a highly sophisticated player.

In a choked-up voice Richie would tell the Au Review how much the band needed to perform this Small World show. "It's the most important show we've ever done, really," he said.

"After the death of our brother, our band mate and our soul spirit Jay only three weeks ago, this gig was already booked. We talked about it and thought it was the perfect opportunity to pay homage and tribute to his life and have our friends and families and fans come along and offer them an opportunity to say goodbye."

As for what happened from that point on, Richie said they weren't in the right place to work out what the band would do now. "We decided to just be cool and make that decision when we're in a better state of mind."

Just after the Small World show, the single *Drop in the Ocean* would come out. The release had already been planned before Jay's death, but Steve said "the song now had more meaning and will be a further tribute to him". Richie would describe the song as "about the power of one, how collectively we are a part of something bigger and better and it is a fitting tribute to Jay."

As is the case with the death of a loved one, there was the realisation that time is fleeting and the need to make a difference now before it's too late. To that end, the band chose to highlight the work of the Sea Shepherd conservation group in the video for the song. "We want to contribute," Richie told Music Feeds, "we want to do what we can to raise awareness about important issues and to highlight and support people who are dedicated to making the world a better place. Life is too short and too precious to waste any more time."

The band would play a couple of shows in Melbourne – with a drawing by Lenny of Jay's bass gracing the gig posters. Still not sure whether they were going to continue they opted for a number of stand-ins on bass, including younger brother Mick Curley, his HyTest bandmate Luke Armstrong (who was taught how to play bass by Jay) and Wally Meanie from The Meanies.

23

After that handful of Melbourne shows near the end of 2014, the band would be honoured as part of an exhibition exploring a half-century of music in Wollongong. Held at the Wollongong Art Gallery, *Steel City Sound* would devote a section solely to the band's memorabilia, which included a Tumbleweed pinball machine. The band would keep a low profile in the first half of 2015; Richie would do a solo show and Lenny would have his first-ever solo art show.

But things were going on behind the scenes. That year was the 20th anniversary of *Galactaphonic* and Tumbleweed approached Universal Music about the idea of putting out a commemorative version.

Universal was keen (thanks in large part to the guy in charge of the label's back catalogue being a huge Tumbleweed fan) and so on August 7, the "20th anniversary Supergalactaphonic Edition" was released. As well as the original album, it came with a bonus disc of B-sides, rarities and live tracks (most sourced from Steve's large collection of tape recordings of the band kept in his archives) – making it 34 songs all together. The release would also see the band hitting the road again, though they still weren't over Jay's death. Curley family friend Armstrong would fill-in on bass duties again, but he wasn't a full-time member. "Replacing Jay is not really an option we want to consider right now," Richie told the Something You Said website. "As for Luke taking on the duties, he's perfect for it. Luke still has Bruce! and HyTest and other projects as well so we're all fitting things in around everyone's commitments."

But they were no longer quite so clear on whether they were going to bring the curtain down on Tumbleweed.

"The band is something we've been doing our whole lives and it's difficult to let go," Richie told me in 2015. "At this moment we're taking it project by project and taking it easy. It's hard to know where it's going to go, it's [Jay's death] certainly changed things a lot in terms of how we feel about it." He added that, as long as they kept enjoying playing with each other and it remained interesting, they'd probably stick at it.

Since the reformation, they had been playing some *Galactaphonic* songs – such as *Hang Around* and *Nothin' to do With the Weather* – in the live shows. But Richie said the band wasn't passing their spare time listening to their old albums; he would compare it to looking at yourself in a mirror; "you can do it for a short amount of time but you're not going to stand there looking at yourself in the mirror for too long". But they would have to listen to *Galactaphonic*, for their latest tour would see them playing the album from start to finish.

"There are [songs] like *This'll Be The End of Me* or *Jupiter* or *Feed The River*," he said. "These are songs that I haven't heard for years and years and years. I'm looking forward to playing these songs the most because they're new and fresh." Especially *Feed The River* it seems; that was a song Richie didn't much care for back in the day but he liked more now.

The tour would take them to Wollongong, as well as other places like Sydney, Melbourne, Brisbane, Adelaide and Perth through August and September 2015. And then they would disappear from view.

24

For all intents and purposes, it looked like Tumbleweed were over. They may have been planning to quietly drift off, just like they did the first time they called it quits, but then Richie's Hot Rollers bandmate Kram asked for a favour in early 2017. His band Spiderbait had a series of gigs lined up for the anniversary of their *Ivy and The Big Apples* album and he wanted Tumbleweed on the bill.

"I said, 'no, we haven't got a bassplayer'," Richie remembers.

"He said 'can you just do something for this?'. So we had a meeting about it and said we'd have a jam with Jamie [Cleaves], who was in the Pink Fits with Lenny and just go and do these shows.

"But Jamie just clicked. If it had been anyone else, it probably wouldn't have worked, but he just locked into that position so well both personality-wise and playing-wise.

"And he and Jay had been close as well, they were good bass buddies. So it seemed like a natural thing to go on with Jamie.

"He came at a time to help us digest what had happened and see it through with respect to Jay."

After those Spiderbait shows there would be a handful of other gigs through 2017 – including a few support slots with Wolfmother. Some surprising additions to the setlist would start appearing during those shows. While everything up to the *Galactaphonic* album had been fair game for the revitalised Tumbleweed, contemplating adding tracks from *Return to Earth* or *Mumbo Jumbo* – which neither Paul or Steve played on – seemed a step too far.

And yet the band would introduce *Fang It* into the repertoire and the popular *Silver Lizard*. "That to me, and I think to Lenny as well, was a wonderful gesture from Paul and Steve," Richie said. "For a while it was like 'we're not touching that shit', but we got to a point where they went 'okay, that's popular with people, we'd better learn those songs'.

"They just decided to get to a point where we move on from it, and I think they also brought something to it, they gave [those songs] a slight angle, a slight nuance that they didn't have before."

The arrival of Jamie on bass would get the band looking towards recording something new, but giving it a different slant now that any new songs weren't going to be heard on Triple J. Nor would there be an attempt to sound cool for the kids. "That's not going to be part of our group manifesto," Richie told me in early 2018.

The idea would be to head to Jamie's house in the Illawarra's northern suburbs and record a few tracks over a weekend. What would happen with the songs from that point didn't seem to have been nailed down.

"It's more about getting in a room and experimenting and seeing where things go," Richie told me. "Recording seven-inch vinyl for ourselves and our fans. Maybe do 500 copies of new songs and then putting it out. Once we've got that sort of thing going we could release it digitally.

"We're aiming to be a bit more prolific and a little bit more productive with the songs rather than feel we have to rush to get an album out."

The decision to talk about new songs might have been a reaction to scoring a series of Day on the Green shows alongside other bands from the days of old, like Spiderbait, Veruca Salt, The Lemonheads and The Fauves. While the band was happy to stand up onstage and play the "greatest hits" set to the old fans who now had kids and couldn't stay up late anymore, Richie wanted to make sure people knew that was only part of what Tumbleweed was.

"You separate yourself a little bit," he said. "There's the creative side of the band, where it's important to remain as creatively vibrant and relevant and fulfill creative urges to write songs, do new things and explore new territories. That is still part of being a collective as a band.

"At the same time we've got this 30-year history as a band in this country, and we still really enjoy going out and playing our 'best of' set to those people who love it."

The big thing on the Tumbleweed calendar for 2018 wasn't anything new; rather it was something very old. Jeb Taylor from Music Farmers record store and label Farmer and the Owl had been talking with the band about releasing the self-titled debut on vinyl. The idea was to get it out a year earlier in 2017 – the 25th anniversary of the 1992 release – but they missed the boat.

After chatting with Stavrakis from Waterfront, they got it going for Record Store Day on April 13, 2018. As well as seeing the *Tumbleweed* album on vinyl for the first time, there would also be the limited edition vinyl single release of *Daddy Long Legs*.

"Tumbleweed are a really important part of the Wollongong music story," Taylor said. "Personally I probably wouldn't be working in music if it wasn't for Tumbleweed. As a very young teenager I discovered a couple of songs from the band and when I realised they were a bunch of guys from a few suburbs down the road, doing well on the national stage, it was an inspiration to me. First to start a high school band and play shows and from doing that, it led me into the music scene and booking venues, managing bands, opening a record shop and starting a record label."

The band had liked *Galactaphonic* more than their debut, which is part of the reason the second album's re-release happened ahead of the first. *Tumbleweed* might be the fans' favourite album but the band didn't think it sounded like them. And some of the songs were banged together in a bit of a rush.

"Our debut album came out at the tail-end of our most fertile and productive period," Richie told TheMusic.com.au. "We had recorded *Theatre of Gnomes* and *WeedSeed* that year and by the time we got to recording the album, our bag of songs was looking pretty bare. We had about six or so that we were already playing live and a few of them we had saved for the album but we needed more. We wrote the remainder in a writing frenzy in the week leading up to the recording."

Most things mellow with time, including the band's feelings towards the release. Listening to it 26 years later, Richie said it was almost like he could pretend he was listening to someone else. And they would have to listen to it, because they were going to play the album live in the tiny Music Farmers shop on Keira Street for

Record Store Day.

"It's been an interesting process listening to it again and getting ready to play it live from beginning to end," Richie said. "A lot of those songs [including *A Darkness at Never Never* and both *Dandylions*] we didn't even do live."

YouTube has footage of the show, which Richie was worried would be seen as a bunch of "old farts" taking up space in the store. Instead, the small crowd on the day appreciated the gig and the band were hassled by fans who missed out, so they took the first album show on the road. The Brisbane show at The Triffid was recorded and there was talk about releasing it as a live album, but as of mid-2020 it still had not seen the light of day.

"It was great playing the first album from start to finish," Richie told *Forte*. "It was a different dynamic; where our usual live set is constructed around building the intensity as we go, with the album set, it was kind of peppered in light and shade."

While the *Tumbleweed* tour was under way, the band got into a bit of cross-promotional synergy via Geelong beer brewer Valhalla. Launched onto the market was Galactaphonic Tonic (Richie came up with the name), a "juicy pale ale" in a can modelled after the *Galactaphonic* album artwork. The beer came about after Steve got an email from a fan who'd been to a

Day on the Green show at Geelong but missed the chance to buy a Tumbleweed T-shirt. Steve noted the words "Valhalla Brewing" in the email address and made a deal to swap some shirts for some beer. The guy at the other end – who was brewer Scott Hunt – paid for the shirts, and then sent some beer up anyway.

"I was a fan of Tumbleweed back in the '90s," Hunt said to me. "I remember seeing them at ANU in Canberra in 1992. My wife and I were originally planning on opening a bar in Perth back in 2002 and we were going to name it after one of Tumbleweed's songs, *Silver Lizard*, but that never happened."

A few weeks after that initial email exchange, Hunt touched base again and asked if Tumbleweed were interested in putting out a beer.

"I'd been looking to do something a bit different," Hunt said. "The craft beer industry is very collaborative. A lot of breweries will do beers together but I wanted to look outside the industry to do collaborations and thought it would be great to do a collaboration with a band."

In late September 2018, after touring the re-release of the first album, the question was raised again – how about a *new* album. Richie said the band still wasn't keen on a whole album, because you put all that effort into songs at the back end of the disc and no one listens to them, they just want the singles. Instead,

Richie said the latest plan was to release nothing but singles. "We are keen to do new stuff and have been writing new songs and I am excited about where they could go, but we think the best way to do it is to record a couple of songs at a time and release limited edition vinyl singles, available via subscription."

Then, at the end of the year, the best recordings would become an album. But there was still no word on when this would actually happen.

They would close out 2018 with an appearance at Wollongong's Yours & Owls festival and a gig that made Steve very happy – a support slot with UK garage rock band Pretty Things. While he was in The Unheard (pre-Tumbleweed), the band would perform a cover of a cover of a Pretty Things tune. They'd heard Australian garage band The Wild Colonials do a version of the Pretty Things' *Get The Picture* but, given this was the 1980s and the internet didn't exist, they hadn't heard the original. One day, Steve managed to find the album, found the original tune was dirtier and slower and was instantly hooked.

He was so hooked in fact, that he'd once end up leaving a gig at Wollongong's Oxford Tavern and driving to another gig in Melbourne after hearing a rumour that Pretty Things bassplayer John Stax might get up onstage. "We jumped in Tom Dion's 1965 Ford Falcon and drove the nine hours overnight down the

Hume Highway," Steve told TheMusic.com.au. "I remember the gig but don't recall how I got home but I was back in the Gong by Sunday arvo slightly worse for wear."

25

October 31, 2019, marked the 10th anniversary of the Tumbleweed reformation. That meant Mark II had been together longer than Mark I. And the band would be promising big things in store over the next two years.

For starters, 2020 should finally see the release of the first of those planned series of singles that Richie first spoke of in 2018. That first single had already been decided on by late 2019. One side was "quite punk", Richie said, while the other was "a little bit complex". The delay seems in part due to the ongoing impacts of COVID-19, and also that the band had to get used to doing things on a smaller scale – the songs are being recorded in Jamie's home studio.

"It's been a long time coming," Richie admitted in the back end of 2019. "We've always tended to record big – big producer, big studio – and spend a lot of money. We've never done it where we've actually been the producers and set up the recording ourselves. Jamie's quite good at recording so we're building up to do our home recording – we're going to do it all ourselves."

Following on from that the plan is to release a single a month working towards 2021, which will be the 30th anniversary of the band's formation back in 1991. Fans will also be able to buy a box to put their 10 singles in, and they'll also all go on to be released as an album. On top of that, there could be a live album in the offing. "There is a live record waiting to go, so we've got to sort that out," Richie said. "We did a recording of Tumbleweed in CBGBs when we played there – which Jack Endino mixed – that's just been sitting there. I think the only salvageable thing there is *Interstellar Overdrive* – I'd like to get that out too."

And then there's talk of a documentary and a coffee table book on the band's history. Trying to get all of that out over the next 12 months is a big ask – and there's the possibility that coronavirus may have delayed these grand plans.

But, jeez, it'd be great if they did manage it.

Best of

If mixtapes were still a thing and someone asked me to make one of Tumbleweed's best songs, this is what they'd get. Hopefully, it'd all fit on one side of a C90 cassette. If you don't know what that means, just ask your parents.

Fritz. An instrumental the band would open with early in their career. A central point is the bass groove Jay lays down, which drives the song. Sometimes I think the tune sounds like the theme song to a cool 1960s TV show.

Carousel. Just a lovely piece of indie pop. The band made their first video to promote the song; an arty black and white number where the band give their hair a real workout.

Healer. The book takes its name from this song, so you knew it had to appear on this list. But that's not the only reason for it being here. It's the first song that boasts the "Tumbleweed sound". I still can't believe that they released this on a sampler EP and then sat on it for more than a year before redoing it for one of their own releases.

Acid Rain: When Jay passed away in 2014, this is the song the band chose to post on their Facebook page as a memorial to him. Off their debut album it was a sign that those who pegged Tumbleweed as stoner rock had gotten it wrong.

Sundial: What Tumbleweed best-of wouldn't include at least one song with marijuana references? It no doubt caused plenty of confusion back in the day when people went into the record store asking for a song called "Mary Jane".

Daddy Long Legs: Starts with such a big, huge, thick guitar riff – it's like they played it on 50 different guitars and layered them one on top of the other for this single. Man, it's just so dense. Yet what lies underneath is a great pop song. If someone recorded it with a cleaner guitar that would be obvious to people.

Hang Around: For a while this was my favourite Tumbleweed song, so much so that I got a little excited at the fact the *Galactaphonic* 20th anniversary release came with three versions. Now something else on this list is my favourite – but this is still a stonking good song. Strange video though. Why is the band being chased by a giant chicken?

Lava Bread: The band certainly lost something when Paul and Steve were shown the door, but that doesn't mean everything was lacklustre. This track from the *Return to Earth* album is a real swinger. Vintage Tumbleweed.

Silver Lizard: Yeah, it's a good song but it shows what happened when Steve left the band. This song is crying out for the swing his drumming so often brought to the band. The reformed line-up plays the song now, but Steve is locked into playing the way it sounds on the record – which probably isn't how he'd have played it if he was part of its creation.

Midnight Sunshine: I appreciate what Tumbleweed was trying to do on the *Mumbo Jumbo* album but they didn't really pull it off. It ended up as a patchy collection of tunes, sounding like a band who knew what they didn't want to be any more but wasn't clear on where to go. That said, there is still a gem or two to be found, such as this lovely, gentle slightly Beatlesque tune.

Mandlebrot: This is off the band's first album in about 12 years, and was a great way to kick things off. It just gets you excited to see what else the album has in store. It has the Tumbleweed DNA, but with the addition of a few extra strands to show the members developed in that decade they were defunct.

Mountain: Someone needs to book them to play in an arena. Cause that's where this song needs to be played to give it the full effect. A huge song needs a huge venue.

Drop in the Ocean: And we close things off with the best song the band has ever released. Screw the fact it's not the usual Tumbleweed "sound", it's tender, uplifting and lets you wrap yourself up in it. It's just frigging beautiful. No matter how much attention it gets, it will never get the attention it deserves.

Bibliography

Books

Humphries, Glen, *Friday Night at the Oxford*, Last Day of School, 2018

Mathieson, Craig, *The Sell-in: How the Music Business Seduced Alternative Rock*, Allen & Unwin, 2000

McFarlane, Ian, *The Encyclopedia of Australian Rock and Pop* (2nd ed), Third Stone Press, 2017

Walker, Clinton, *Stranded: The Secret History of Australian Independent Music 1977-1991*, Pan Macmillan, 1996

Newspapers/magazines

Adie, Kilmeny, 'Soulmates band together', *Illawarra Mercury*, December 17, 1998

'Alternative group finds its niche', *Illawarra Mercury*, May 26, 1989

Boulton, Martin, 'Born from the Sabbath', *The Age*, November 23, 2012

Boulton, Martin, Ready to roll out new tunes', *The Age*, May 25, 2012

Cosgrove, Shady, 'Sounds of the South', *Illawarra Mercury*, February 27, 1999

Crabb, Brendan, 'Tumbleweed moves on', *Lake Times*, November 27, 2013

Dalton, Rodney, 'Blakeley brings soulful sounds to steel city', *Illawarra Mercury*, June 28, 1990

Dixon, Craig, 'Mumbo Jumbo review', *The Age*, June 30, 2000

Fontaine, Angus, 'Tumbling happily back to Earth', *Daily Telegraph*, August 22, 1996

Gostelow, Ian, 'Tumbleweed', *Independent Music Monthly*, January 1994

Gregory, Helen, 'Right back rolling along again', *Newcastle Herald*, December 27, 2010

Gregory, Helen, 'Rolling back for more', *Newcastle Herald*, January 18, 2014

Gregory, Helen, 'Where the wind blows', *Newcastle Herald*, January 6, 2011

'High-energy Protons achieve chart success', Illawarra Mercury, May 18, 1990

Hitchings, Stuart, 'The killer Weed', *Juice*, 1995

Holmes, Peter, 'Up Like Weeds', *Sun-Herald*, July 23, 1995

Humphries, Glen, 'A new take on old songs', *Illawarra Mercury*, July 21, 2015

Humphries, Glen, 'Band will perform in honour of Curley', *Illawarra Mercury*, September 2, 2014

Humphries, Glen, 'Debut creeping along', *Illawarra Mercury*, January 27, 2005

Humphries, Glen, 'Gyroscope on the Blink tour again', *Illawarra Mercury*, June 23, 2004

Humphries, Glen, 'Here come the Sundial', *Illawarra Mercury*, March 31, 2018

Humphries, Glen, 'Monstrous summer', *Illawarra Mercury*, September 19, 2003

Humphries, Glen, 'Out of the Blue', *Illawarra Mercury*, February 13, 2003

Humphries, Glen, 'Posse rides out as a unit', *Illawarra Mercury*, September 23, 2013

Humphries, Glen, 'Riding out the Tumbleweed roller-coaster', *Illawarra Mercury*, November 15, 2008

Humphries, Glen, 'Rolling out new tunes', *Illawarra Mercury*, March 29, 2012

Humphries, Glen, 'Taking a tumble', *Illawarra Mercury*, November 15, 2008

Humphries, Glen, 'Tragic loss of loved musician', *Illawarra Mercury*, August 27, 2014

Humphries, Glen, 'Tumbleweed Mark II', *Illawarra Mercury*, December 16, 2010

Humphries, Glen, 'Tumbleweed rollin' back', *Illawarra Mercury*, October 31, 2009

'Inside the 1992 Nirvana tour with support act

Tumbleweed', *HMV Massive* magazine, July 2000

Johnson, Daniel, 'Gong way to the top', *Courier-Mail*, July 8, 2018

Johnson, Daniel, 'Sounds From the Other Side' review, *Courier-Mail*, November 23, 2013

Johnson, Lisa, 'Tumbleweed heads Condofest line-up', *Illawarra Mercury*, November 1992

Karen (sic), 'An interview with Lenny from Tumbleweed', *Independent Music Monthly*, November 1994

Lazarevic, Jade, 'Tumbling back into the spotlight', *Newcastle Herald*, April 7, 2012

Long, Ben, 'Rockers all grown up', *Illawarra Mercury*, January 11, 2013

Maloney, Matt, 'Tumbleweed blows back into Hobart', *The Mercury*, January 23, 2014

Maloney, Matt, 'Tumbleweed blows back into town', *Launceston Examiner*, June 3, 2011

Messenger, ICT, 'Tumbleweed', *B-Side Magazine*

Neilson, Mark, 'Pop goes the Weed', *Drum Media*, June 14, 1990

Mathieson, Craig, 'Tumbleweed keep rolling on', *Sydney Morning Herald*, August 21, 2015

McUtchen, Andrew 'Brothers are doin' it', *Herald Sun*, January 1, 1998

McUtchen, Andrew, 'Weeds pop up again', *Herald Sun*, October 17, 1996

'Men and their machines', *Hot Metal*, 1997

Molitorisz, Sacha, 'Weed the world', *Sydney Morning Herald*, November 1, 1996

Moore, Chris, 'Tumbleweed's on track', *Illawarra Mercury*, August 3, 2000

Moore, Chris, 'Tumbleweed rolls again', *Illawarra Mercury*, April 13, 2000

Nicholson, Geoff, 'White anxiety', *Time Off Magazine*, 1998

'Nightlife', *Illawarra Mercury*, September 7, 1989

'Q&A with Lenny Curley', *Newcastle Herald*, January 20, 2000

'Ready to tumble', *Canberra Times*, January 13, 2011

'Re-emergence of the Weed, *The Advertiser*, October 24, 1996

Rocca, Jane, 'Weed smoking again', *The Age*, May 29, 1998

Rockman, Lisa, 'The Weed spark a '90s alt-rock revival', *Newcastle Herald*, September 1, 2018

Savage, Desiree, 'Wollongong '90s band Tumbleweed touring with Wolfmother', *Illawarra Mercury*, April 13, 2017

Simpson, Nathan, 'Tumbleweed reborn', *Wollongong Advertiser*, October 28, 2009

'The Pills find the energy to win contract', *Illawarra Mercury*, February 9, 1989

Thomas, Brett, 'We're no tumbling hippies', *Sun-*

Herald, April 23, 1993

Thomson, Owen, 'Tumbleweed energised by proton pills', *Illawarra Mercury*, December 1990

Turk, Louise, 'Tumbleweed guitarist performs solo show', *Illawarra Mercury*, July 18, 2015

Vincent, Craig, 'Staging tribute for Jay', *Illawarra Mercury*, September 19, 2014

Vincent, Craig, 'Tumbleweed's Jason Curley dies suddenly', *Sydney Morning Herald*, August 26, 2014

Vincent, Craig, 'Tumbleweed may hang up guitars', *Sydney Morning Herald*, September 19, 2014

Yates, Rod, Return of the Weed', *Drum Media*, November 9, 1999

Waters, Kim, 'Zambian Goat Herders', *Independent Music Monthly*, February 1994

Watson, Chad, 'Weed and wonderful', *Newcastle Herald*, July 27, 2000

Weber, Dave '200 questions with Dave Curley', *Independent Music Monthly*, February 1995

'Weed are the champions', *Drum Media*, October 1996

Young, Kane, 'Acid Rain to reign again', *The Mercury*, May 26, 2011

Zalunardo, Paul, 'Tumbleweed praises local scene', *Illawarra Mercury*, April 16, 1998

Websites

Apter, Jeff, 'Weed scene', Sydney Morning Herald, September 18, 2013

Emery, Patrick, 'Tumbleweed', Beat magazine, Hennessy, Kate, 'Tumbleweed – icon series', Mess + Noise, December 2009

Hohnen, Mike, 'Tumbleweed chat new album and getting the gang back together', Music Feeds, October 10, 2013

Hollick, Michael, 'Get ready to Tumble' X-Press music magazine

Hunter, Chelsea, 'Tumbleweed: We aint got the technology', Bluestar Media, 2000

'Interview -Richie Lewis, Tumbleweed', 100% Rock Magazine, September 2015

'Interview with Richie Lewis from Tumbleweed', Tomatrax online music magazine, July 2015

Laird, Bruce, 'Tumbleweed', Beat magazine

Leigh [sic], 'Richie Lewis (Tumbleweed) interview 2010', Digging a Hole, June 19, 2010

Steel City Sound, 'Independent Music Monthly', March 3, 2012

Steel City Sound, 'The Proton Energy Pills', September 7, 2010

Steel City Sound, 'Zambian Goat Herders', April 2010

'Tumbleweed take a trip back to '92', Forte,

September 24, 2018

'Tumbleweed embrace the beauty', Something You Said, August 2015

'*Tumbleweed* track by track with Richie Lewis and Lenny Curley', TheMusic.com.au, July 3, 2018

Williams, Tom, 'Tumbleweed announce SuperGalactaphonic national tour', Music Feeds, 2015

Wood, Chris, 'In the Ghetto with Tumblweed', The Dwarf, October 16, 2009Th

Young, David James, 'Tumbleweed are gearing up for a milestone tour', Beat magazine

Videos

'Episode 1: Tumbleweed', Helter Smelter TV, 2012

'Interview: Richie Lewis of Tumbleweed', Parts 1 and 2, The Au Review 2013

'Interview with Richie Lewis of Tumbleweed', InMidAir-Music 2010

Richard Lewis of Tumbleweed: Interview at Young Henrys Small World Festival', The Au Review, 2014

Music

Proton Energy Pills
Rocket to Tarrawanna, Bang, 2006

Tumbleweed (in chronological order)
Captain's Log single, Waterfront *1992*
Weedseed, Waterfront, 1992
Theatre of Gnomes, Waterfront, 1992
Tumbleweed, Waterfront, 1992
Sundial single 1992
Daddy Long Legs single, Waterfront, 1993
Galactaphonic, Polydor, 1995
Return to Earth, Polydor, 1996
Fang It single, Polydor, 1998
Mumbo Jumbo, Grudge, 2000
The Waterfront Years, Aztec Music, 2010
Sounds From the Other Side, Shock, 2013
Galactaphonic 20th anniversary release, Universal, 2015

Related bands
Richie and the Creeps, *Richie and the Creeps*, Illustrious Artists, 2007
The Monstrous Blues, *Colourblind*, High Beam Music, 2003
The Monstrous Blues, *A Pocket Full of Moon Rocks*, Impendence Records, 2009

[Glen Humphries]

The Pink Fits, *De Ja Blues*, Off The Hip
The Pink Fits, *Fuzzyard Gravebox*, Off The Hip
Zambian Goat Herders, *Endorphin*, Redback Music,
1993

Lightning Source UK Ltd.
Milton Keynes UK
UKHW010627051020
371035UK00001B/73